The story of
FLIGHT

by John Lewellen, Irwin Shapiro and Maurice Allward

Hamlyn
London New York Sydney Toronto

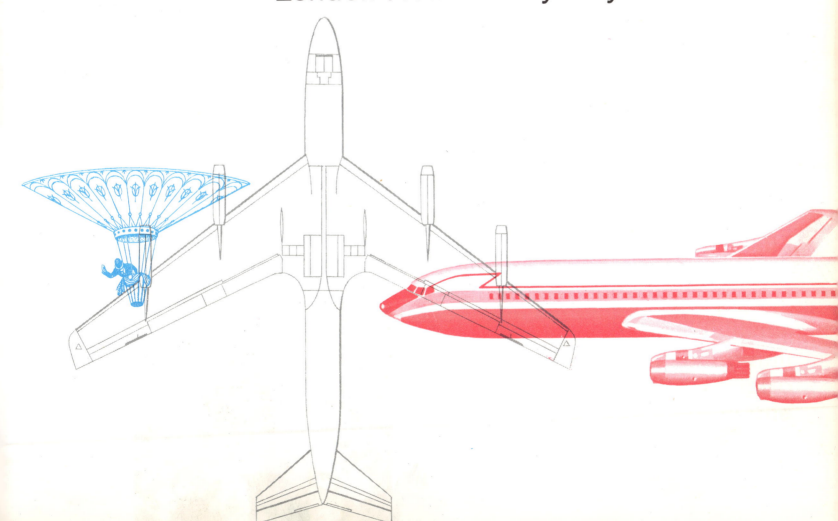

CONTENTS

First published 1970
Second impression 1972
Published by The Hamlyn Publishing Group Limited
London · New York · Sydney · Toronto
Hamlyn House, Feltham, Middlesex, England
for Golden Pleasure Books Limited
© Copyright Western Publishing Company Inc., 1959
All rights reserved
Printed in Great Britain by Cox & Wyman, Fakenham
ISBN 0 601 08663 5

Nike, the Greek goddess of victory.

Winged lion of the Middle Ages.

Khonsu, an Egyptian winged god.

The Flying throne of Kai Ka'us of Persia.

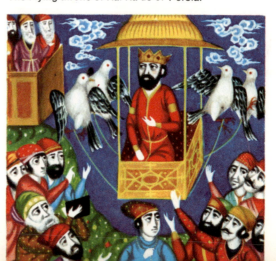

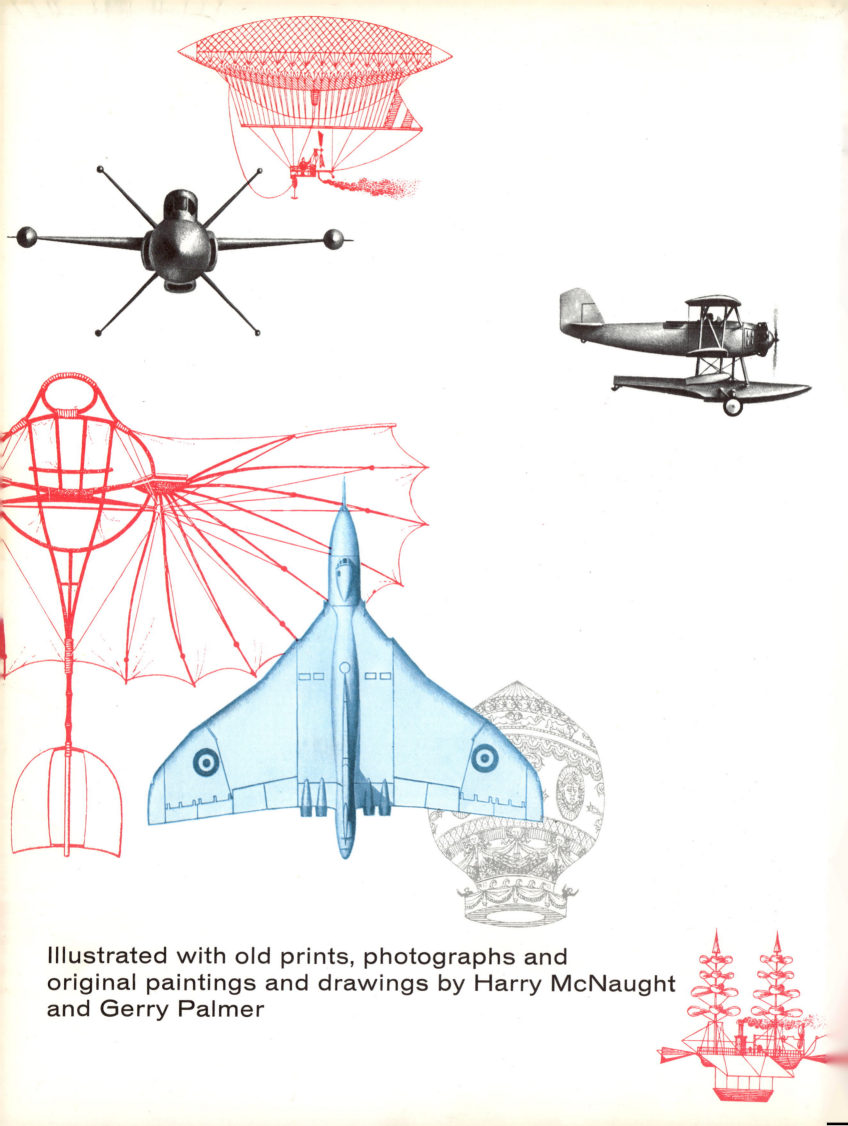

Illustrated with old prints, photographs and
original paintings and drawings by Harry McNaught
and Gerry Palmer

The story of Daedalus and Icarus is an old Greek legend.

Tower jumper of the eleventh century.

BIRDS, GODS, DEVILS AND MEN

Thousands of years ago, even before the days of written history, men looked up at the birds in the sky. They might have been Babylonians, Assyrians, Egyptians, Greeks. For everywhere in all countries, men watched the birds and longed to fly. But men were creatures of the earth. True, they had learnt to get about on water as well as on land. They could travel by rivers and over lakes and seas. But to their great frustration they could not voyage in the great ocean of air above the earth. Gods might do it, perhaps, and devils. But not men.

And so men gave wings to their gods and devils, in pictures, statues, and stories. Some could fly by magic, without wings. Some rode flying horses, goats, tigers,

lions, bulls, and dragons. Others rode through the air in chariots or boats, pulled by flying beasts.

One of the oldest stories of flying was told by the Greeks. It was about Daedalus and his son, Icarus. To escape from the island of Crete, they fastened wings of feathers to themselves with wax. Daedalus flew to Sicily. But Icarus came too close to the sun, and the wax melted. He fell into the sea and was drowned.

In the eleventh century, some men did actually try to fly. They strapped wing-like devices to their arms and legs, and jumped off high towers and cliffs. Most of them were killed or badly crippled.

The air still belonged to the gods and the devils— and to the swift, soaring birds.

7

Leonardo da Vinci made many sketches for flying machines in his notebooks.

CHALLENGE FROM THE SKY

Time went on, and many things changed in the world. But men did not lose their longing to fly. Always there were birds winging across the sky, challenging men to discover their secret. And one of the men who took up the challenge was Leonardo da Vinci.

Leonardo was a painter, sculptor, architect, musician, engineer, inventor and scientist. There were few fields in which he was not interested. He studied birds carefully, watching how they moved. He studied the air, too. He designed an ornithopter – a flying machine with flapping wings – to be worked by a man's arms and legs. Inspite of all his concentrated study, Leonardo could

not meet the challenge from the sky. His flying machine could not fly. It failed for exactly the same reason that the men who had jumped from towers and cliffs had failed. Man's muscles are simply not strong enough to lift him by flapping wings. And even with an engine for power, the flying machine would not have worked. Leonardo constructed the pair of wings so that they flapped downward and back. His trouble was that he never learnt that birds flap their wings downward and *forward*.

Inspite of his mistakes, however, Leonardo was the first real scientist in the history of flight. Unfortunately, after his death in 1519, his writings on flying were lost to the world for several hundred years. Not until 1797 did they become known to other scientists, who immediately appreciated their value.

Meanwhile, in 1670, an Italian priest, Francesco de Lana, took up the challenge. It was the air itself, rather than the birds, that particularly interested him. Father Francesco knew that the air has a definite weight. Then why couldn't something lighter than air float upward, like a cork bobbing up in the water? It certainly sounded possible.

'Why not, indeed?' Father Francesco thought, and he set about designing an airship. The body was like a boat, with a mast and a sail. Attached to the boat were four hollow globes of very thin copper, from which the air had been removed. The globes would then rise up from the ground, carrying the boat with them gently into the air.

Father Francesco put aside the drawing he had made, and looked out of the window. He could imagine airships sailing in the air, high above the cities of the earth. And he could imagine something else—war from the sky. It was a new, terrible kind of war, more dreadful than anything the world had ever known. He could almost hear the crash of falling buildings, the roar and crackle of flames, the shrieks and cries of the dying.

Picking up his pen, he wrote, in great agitation: 'Who can fail to see that no city would be proof against surprise, when the ship could be steered over its squares, or even over the courtyards of dwelling houses, and brought to earth for the landing of its crew?...... Iron weights could be hurled to wreck ships at sea, or they could be set on fire by fireballs and bombs; not ships alone, but houses, fortresses and cities could thus be destroyed, with the certainty that the airship could come to no harm as the missiles would be hurled from a vast height.'

But it would be many years before there would be war from the sky. Father Francesco's airship was never built. If it had been built, it would never have left the ground. The weight of the outside air would have crushed the globes of thin copper. And, since the airship would have moved with the air in which it floated, the sail would have been useless.

And yet, like Leonardo's flying machine which did not fly, Father Francesco's airship was an important step forward in the story of flight. It helped show the way to men who would some day outfly the birds, travelling through the sky like the gods and devils of old.

A flying boat, as imagined by Francesco de Lana in 1670.

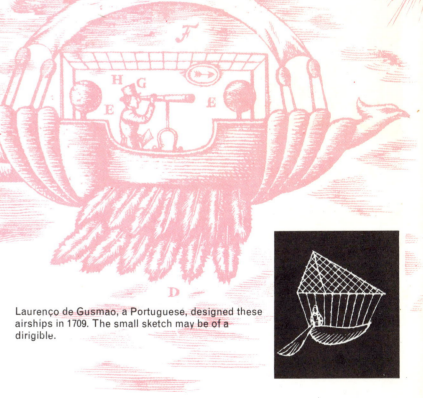

Laurenço de Gusmao, a Portuguese, designed these airships in 1709. The small sketch may be of a dirigible.

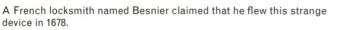

A French locksmith named Besnier claimed that he flew this strange device in 1678.

The first manned balloon flight.

A CLOUD IN A BAG

Early design for a powered balloon by Besnier.

In the year 1782, in the town of Annonay in France, there lived two brothers. They were called Joseph and Etienne Montgolfier. Often the brothers looked up at the sky. High above them, higher than the trees, higher than the church steeple, floated the clouds. They drifted with the wind, like great white ships of the air.

The brothers agreed how nice it would be to float on a cloud. But a cloud was just vapour, lighter than air. If they could only capture a cloud in a big bag, it would rise and carry them with it. Actually, they would not even need a cloud. They could use any substance lighter than air. It was essential to find something.

The days passed, and the brothers could find no answer. Then, one cold winter night, they were sitting near the fireplace in the kitchen. They noticed that smoke and bits of ash floated upward from the fire. They might not be able to capture a cloud, but they could catch a bagful of smoke. They found a small silk bag and held it over the flames. When they let go, the bag rose.

The brothers tried the experiment again and again, then decided to experiment outdoors with a larger bag. On June 5, 1783, everything was ready. They held a linen bag thirty-eight feet in diameter over a fire of

10

straw. The bag rose 6,000 feet, travelled for ten minutes, and fell to earth a mile and a half away. The Montgolfiers had discovered the balloon.

At first they believed that smoke or a new kind of gas from the fire made the balloon rise. Soon they learnt that the fire merely heated the air in the balloon. Hot air is considerably lighter than cool air, and the balloon floated until the air inside it grew as cool as the air which surrounded it.

The brothers made other experiments. While the king and queen and a great crowd watched, they sent up a balloon that carried a cage of animals. Another time, they sent up a man in a captive balloon—a balloon kept from drifting by ropes held on the ground.

On November 21, 1783, one of their balloons carried Pilâtre de Rozier and the Marquis d'Arlandes, the first men to make a successful flight. A fire in a metal container attached to the balloon kept the air in it hot. The balloon stayed up for twenty-five minutes, floated across Paris, and then landed gently five and a half miles away.

Only ten days later, another kind of balloon was ready to take to the air. It was designed by a French physicist, Professor J. A. C. Charles. It was made of rubber-coated silk by two brothers named Robert, and was filled with hydrogen gas instead of hot air.

Hydrogen had been discovered in 1766 by Henry Cavendish, an English chemist. It was the lightest substance known, weighing much less than air. But before Professor Charles, no one had thought of using it in a balloon.

Professor Charles and the older of the two Robert brothers made the first flight in a hydrogen balloon. They stayed up for two hours, landing twenty-seven miles away from Paris, where they had started.

After that, many more flights were made in both fire balloons and hydrogen balloons. Jean-Pierre Blanchard, a Frenchman, became the first professional balloonist. With Dr. John Jeffries, an American, he made the first crossing of the English Channel in 1785.

That was the year, too, of the first fatal balloon accident. It happened when Pilâtre de Rozier also tried to cross the Channel. He used a combination of both types of balloons, attaching a small fire balloon below a larger hydrogen balloon. Twenty minutes after he took off with his companion, P. A. de Romain, the hydrogen balloon caught fire. Both men fell 3,000 feet and were killed.

But the balloon flights went on, and in 1793 Blanchard made the first flight in America. George Washington was in the crowd that watched him rising miraculously over Philadelphia.

Men were finding their way to the sky at last.

An 1801 idea for a powered airship.

Cutaway view of a typical gas balloon, showing the envelope, usually made of silk or linen, encased in net webbing. Hanging from the passenger basket are sandbags used as ballast.

January 1785. Jean Pierre Blanchard and Dr. John Jeffries make the first aerial crossing of the Channel in a balloon equipped with rudder and aerial oars.

First successful dirigible in the history of flight was built in 1852 by Henri Giffard. Steering by means of a sail at rear of craft, he flew for seventeen miles before coming down.

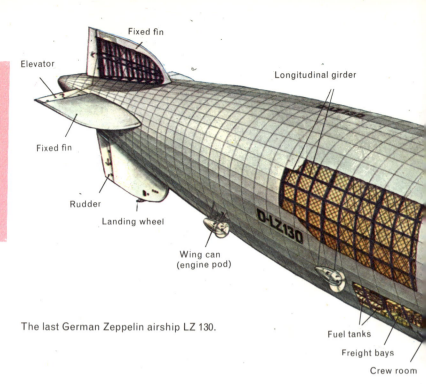

Fixed fin

Elevator

Longitudinal girder

Fixed fin

Rudder

Landing wheel

Wing can (engine pod)

D·LZ·130

Fuel tanks

Freight bays

Crew room

The last German Zeppelin airship LZ 130.

In 1901, Santos-Dumont circled the Eiffel Tower in his 'No. 6' airship.

Huge Zeppelin LZ3, shown in its hangar. The tail-assembly controls guided the airship's altitude and direction. Barrage balloons (right), anchored to the ground, protected cities from low-level bombing in World Wars I and II.

DINOSAURS OF THE AIR

At last men were in the air, floating about like the clouds. And, like the clouds, they could only drift with the wind. There was little they could do to control the balloons. By opening a valve, they could let out the gas and come down. By emptying the sacks of sand they carried, they could lessen the weight on the balloon and rise. And that was all, until the invention of the dirigible.

The dirigible, or airship, as it is also called, is a balloon that can be steered. The first successful one was built in 1852 by Henri Giffard, a French engineer. It was 143 feet long and shaped like a cigar. Attached to it was a three-horsepower steam engine that turned a propeller. Giffard's airship had a speed of about five miles an hour. When it was headed into a wind of the same speed, it remained motionless.

Higher speeds came only with the invention of the lighter and more powerful internal combustion engine. By that time, many balloonists were using coal gas instead of hydrogen for their lifting gas. It was heavier than hydrogen, but cost less. Later, some airships were filled with helium. Although it was also heavier than hydrogen, and much more expensive, it could not catch fire and burn.

Just before the beginning of the twentieth century, two men made airship history. One of them was Alberto Santos-Dumont, a Brazilian who did his flying in France. In 1898 he built his airship, *No. One,* which had a three-and-a-half-horsepower engine. It was the first balloon that could really be guided and controlled.

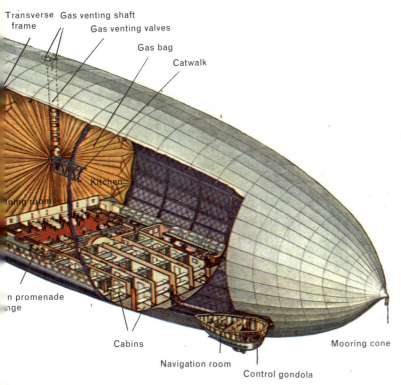

Transverse frame   Gas venting shaft   Gas venting valves   Gas bag   Catwalk   Kitchen   ning room   n promenade   nge   Cabins   Navigation room   Control gondola   Mooring cone

Santos-Dumont built and flew thirteen more airships. Young, daring, likeable, he was a good engineer, a skilful flier, and something of a showman. He seemed as much at home in the air as a bird, and enjoyed floating along the streets of Paris, no higher than the rooftops. He amazed the entire world in 1901 by flying from St. Cloud to the Eiffel Tower, circling the tower, and flying back to St. Cloud.

The other man who made history was Count Ferdinand von Zeppelin, a retired German army officer. In 1898, at the age of sixty, he began building the first of the giant dirigibles that were named after him. It was 420 feet long, the longest balloon ever made. It was also the first rigid balloon, with a framework of aluminium. Hanging from the underside was a cabin for passengers and crew.

Count von Zeppelin used the same idea as Santos-Dumont for getting his ship up and down. Moving a sliding weight backward pointed the nose upward, and the ship rose. Moving the weight forward pointed the nose toward the earth, and the ship came down.

After the success of the first zeppelin, many more were built in Germany. Zeppelins made war from the sky when they dropped bombs on London in World War I. And when the war was over, they crossed the ocean and carried passengers to many parts of the world. The *Graf Zeppelin* made a record flight around the world in 1929, covering 21,700 miles in twenty days and four hours.

Other countries—France, Italy, England, and the

United States—also built huge dirigibles. They became bigger and bigger, faster and faster. Some were as long as 800 feet, with speeds as high as eighty miles an hour.

But meanwhile the aeroplane had been invented and was being improved every year. And dirigibles were hard to handle. Many were lost in accidents. They burned and exploded and were wrecked in storms. On May 6, 1937, the zeppelin *Hindenburg* exploded and burst into flame, and thirty-six persons were killed.

No more of the impressive but clumsy airships were ever built, for they were the dinosaurs of the air. Just as the dinosaurs of prehistoric days gave way to swifter, more clever animals, so the airship gave way to the plane.

Blimps—a smaller, non-rigid type of dirigible—were used for patrol duty in World War I. They did the same work in World War II, and were especially helpful in tracking down submarines. They were also used as barrage balloons. Groups of unmanned blimps, attached to long cables, were left floating in the air to stop low-flying bombing and strafing planes.

After the war, round hydrogen balloons were sent aloft with scientific instruments to gather information on weather. Others, made of plastic, carried men in metal gondolas high into the atmosphere to explore the edge of space. But the monster airships that had once ruled the air were gone.

The explosion of the Zeppelin *Hindenburg* at Lakehurst, N.J.

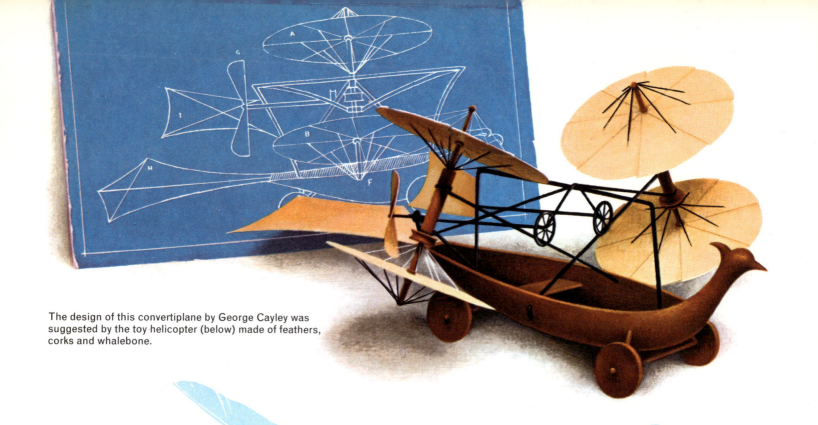

The design of this convertiplane by George Cayley was suggested by the toy helicopter (below) made of feathers, corks and whalebone.

THE MODEL MAKERS

When the Montgolfier brothers sent up the first balloon in 1783, word quickly spread to England. Every boy who heard the news was excited, and one of them was George Cayley.

Ten years later, the boys were grown up. They had other things to think about, and most of them forgot about balloons. George Cayley did not forget. He was Sir George Cayley now, a country gentleman and student of science. Already he had begun the work that would lead to his many inventions, such as the caterpillar tractor, a new type of wheel, and safety devices for railroads. But he never stopped thinking about the problems of flight. He knew that balloons were not the answer. Men would not conquer the air until they learnt the secret of heavier-than-air flight from the birds.

An ordinary kite gave Cayley the idea for the first model of a glider. In 1804, he used a kite as an aircraft wing by attaching it to a pole. He slanted the kite upward to keep the glider from tipping. At one end of the pole he attached a tail unit. This could be adjusted to steer the craft up, down, or sideways. The glider flew, and as Cayley wrote, 'It was very pretty to see it sail down a steep hill'.

Cayley experimented with a number of other gliders. Some were small models, while others were large enough to carry a man. In his notes, he mentioned that one of the larger gliders, with a ten-year-old boy as passenger, 'was floated off the ground for several yards on descending a hill'. It was a great achievement.

Cayley foresaw that aeroplanes of the future would be driven by a propeller instead of by flapping wings. He also foresaw the use of petrol engines to turn the propeller, long before the invention of the internal combustion engine. He made studies of the action of air on wings that were a guide to inventors for years to come. Because of Cayley's many discoveries, he has been called the father of aeronautics.

His last design was for a steam-powered convertiplane—a combination helicopter and aeroplane. It was never built, and it would not have had enough power to get off the ground. But the drawings he made of it in 1843 looked remarkably like the convertiplanes that would be built more than a hundred years later.

The first inventor to use Cayley's ideas was William Henson, an Englishman in the lace-making business. In 1842, aided by John Stringfellow, he designed the *Aerial Steam Carriage*. Henson designed the craft itself, while Stringfellow designed the steam engine. Their plans called for a wing with a span of 150 feet, and an engine of twenty-five to thirty horsepower.

To raise money, the inventors organised the Aerial Transit Company, which would run regularly scheduled flights to all parts of the world. The company was a failure—and so was the plane. Unable to get enough money to build a full-size plane, Henson and Stringfellow built a model with a wingspan of twenty feet. It did not fly, mainly because the engine was too heavy and did not produce enough power.

The two inventors became a great joke to the whole

world. Newspapers made fun of them, and people all over the world laughed at the silly fellows and their crazy schemes. And yet, their plane was amazingly ahead of its time, with many new and unusual features. Years later, aeroplane builders everywhere would copy the wing construction first used in the *Aerial Steam Carriage*.

But Henson was tired of being laughed at. He gave up and settled in America. Stringfellow went on working, and made a model, based on Henson's designs, with a wingspan of ten feet and powered by a steam engine driving twin-pusher airscrews. It was to be launched by an ingenious device attached to a wire. For many years it was thought that this was tested successfully in a lace factory at Chard, in Somerset, and later at Cremorne Gardens, London, in 1848, thus giving Stringfellow the credit for making the first powered aeroplane of history. Recent research, however, indicates that there is no proof that the model left the wire or was capable of powered, sustained, free flight.

Twenty years later Stringfellow made another model, this time a triplane. Although it did not fly properly either, it was proudly exhibited at the Aeronautical Society's Exhibition held at the Crystal Palace in 1868, where it aroused in the public an enormous amount of interest.

Stringfellow's triplane was based on the experiments of Francis Wenham, who built many models of multi-winged gliders during the 1860's. Wenham's gliders did not perform very well in the air. But he learnt many things about the shape of wings and once again a failure brought men closer to discovering the secret of the birds.

Two dirigibles designed by Cayley in 1837.

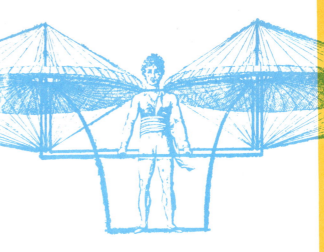

In the early 1800's, 'birdmen' tried to fly with wing-flapping devices like this one. None of them succeeded. Jacob Degen, a Swiss clock-maker, tied a balloon to his apparatus to lighten its weight but was blown helplessly about by wind currents.

Cayley's glider model was made of a kite attached to a pole.

A deserted lace factory at Chard in 1848, scene of Stringfellow's unsuccessful tests on his 10-foot wingspan, steam-powered model.

Imaginary flight of Henson and Stringfellow's *Aerial Steam Carriage*. This
design of 1842 for a powered craft embodied details which later became
standard aeroplane practice. It was never built, but stimulated research.

MORE MODELS AND EXPERIMENTS

Everywhere in Europe and America, newspapers had made fun of Henson and Stringfellow. At the same time, they carried pictures of the *Aerial Steam Carriage* on imaginary flights over strange, far-away places.

Inventors in many countries stared at the pictures, dreaming of the day when such things would come true. What if the steam carriage was a failure! Someone could still win the race to get into the air. And so inventors went on studying, and drawing designs, and building models and making experiments.

In France, in 1871, Alphonse Pénaud built an interesting small model powered by a rubber band. It flew 131 feet in eleven seconds. Four years later, Thomas Moy of England built a huge model he called the *Aerial Steamer*. Two large fans, driven by a steam engine, raised the craft a few inches off the ground. It did not fly, but it made many people believe that steam engines might be used to power aeroplanes.

The following year, something happened that at first seemed to have little to do with flight. It was the invention of the first practical internal combustion engine that used liquid fuel. In time it was improved, until it became the petrol engine, light and powerful enough to be used for aircraft.

Meanwhile, on the other side of the world, an Australian called Lawrence Hargrave was at work. In 1893 he invented the box kite, which suggested the wing design for certain types of gliders and aeroplanes. Horatio Phillips, of England, was also experimenting with wings. He built a curious, steam-powered multiplane, with fifty narrow wings that looked like a Venetian blind. The back wheels rose from the ground when it was tested in 1893.

Another strange plane was tested the following year by Sir Hiram Maxim, an American inventor who made his home in England. It was a four-ton giant, driven on railroad tracks by two 180-horsepower steam engines. The craft was damaged after the wheels lifted from the rails. But Maxim felt that he had solved the most important problems of aviation, and gave up his experiments.

But it was a Frenchman, Clement Ader, who came closest to success. He built several planes with steam engines, and in 1897 he tested his *Avion III*. Although the plane did get off the ground, it hopped rather than flew. Ader can claim to have made the first take-off in a powered aroplane, but only that.

Other inventors kept dreaming, hoping and working, and the race to get into the air went on.

Clement Ader's twin-engined, steam-driven *Avion III* made hops in 1897, but these were too short to constitute true flights.

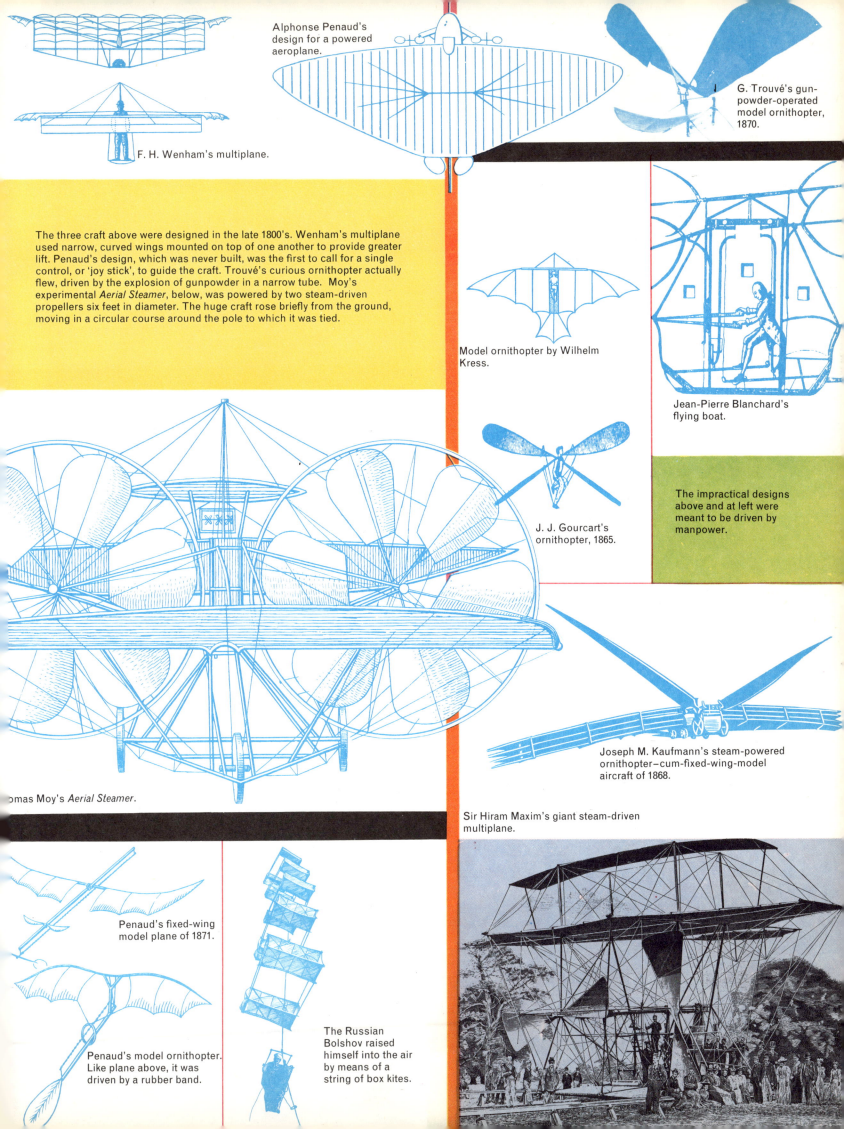

F. H. Wenham's multiplane.

Alphonse Penaud's design for a powered aeroplane.

G. Trouvé's gun-powder-operated model ornithopter, 1870.

The three craft above were designed in the late 1800's. Wenham's multiplane used narrow, curved wings mounted on top of one another to provide greater lift. Penaud's design, which was never built, was the first to call for a single control, or 'joy stick', to guide the craft. Trouvé's curious ornithopter actually flew, driven by the explosion of gunpowder in a narrow tube. Moy's experimental *Aerial Steamer*, below, was powered by two steam-driven propellers six feet in diameter. The huge craft rose briefly from the ground, moving in a circular course around the pole to which it was tied.

Model ornithopter by Wilhelm Kress.

Jean-Pierre Blanchard's flying boat.

J. J. Gourcart's ornithopter, 1865.

The impractical designs above and at left were meant to be driven by manpower.

Thomas Moy's *Aerial Steamer*.

Joseph M. Kaufmann's steam-powered ornithopter–cum–fixed-wing-model aircraft of 1868.

Sir Hiram Maxim's giant steam-driven multiplane.

Penaud's fixed-wing model plane of 1871.

Penaud's model ornithopter. Like plane above, it was driven by a rubber band.

The Russian Bolshov raised himself into the air by means of a string of box kites.

MEN WITH WINGS

Captain Jean-Marie Le Bris stood quietly at the rail of his ship. He was watching an albatross. In all his years at sea, he had never stopped being amazed at these wandering ocean birds. Strange, how they could stay aloft for hours without moving their wings. They rode the air, seeming to hang between the sky and the waves.

That afternoon, Captain Le Bris shot down the big bird. As he studied the wings, he smiled a little. An idea had just come to his mind. It was a wild idea, of course. And yet he kept thinking about it on the voyage home.

Back again in France, Captain Le Bris built an artificial albatross. It was really a glider, made of light wood and cloth. On a windy day in 1857, he put the glider on a farmer's cart. He climbed up into the canoe-shaped body, where there was just room enough for him to stand. While two men ran alongside, steadying the wings, the farmer drove the cart down a country road. Faster and faster it went – and the glider rose.

Captain Le Bris tried to release the rope that held the glider to the cart. It tangled itself around the shouting farmer, pulling him into the air. For a minute or two the glider flew. Then it crashed to the ground.

Le Bris then attempted a launch over a quarry. During the attempt he got caught in a gust of wind and crashed, breaking his leg. Unfortunately, by then he had run out of money and was unable to build any more gliders at that time.

However, he was very popular and ten years later his friends organised a public subscription in Brest which enabled him to build a second 'artificial albatross'

Captain Jean-Marie le Bris launched his glider from a cart. He modelled it on the albatrosses he had watched at sea.

glider. This seems to have made a number of successful flights – with ballast on board instead of a pilot. Encouraged, he made preparations to fly it himself. At the last minute his friends persuaded him not to try, and so he agreed to launch the machine unmanned. It went into a steep climb, turned and then crashed back on to the ground.

This really was the end for Le Bris, for, with his funds exhausted a second time, he did not try to fly again.

Le Bris was no scientist. He did not understand what made his gliders rise, and was ignorant of the important pioneering aeronautical work that had been carried out up to that time. However, he was a brave and colourful pioneer whose claim to history is that he was the first glider pilot. It is sad to record that, after serving honourably in the war of 1870, he became a policeman in which capacity he was killed in 1872 by bandits.

But there were others besides Captain Le Bris who had watched birds flying. In Germany, a boy named Otto Lilienthal was growing up. At the age of thirteen he tried to fly with flapping wings. He and his brother Gustav experimented at night, so that their friends would not see them and laugh.

When he grew up he became an engineer, but his interest in flying increased. He spent years studying the flight of birds, and in 1889 published the important book *Bird Flight as a Basis of Aviation*. In this book he recommended, like the other pioneers Cayley, Wenham and Phillips, cambered wings for the greatest lift. Lilienthal was the first person ever to realise that a bird is propelled forward *not* by beating its wings rearward, but by the propeller-like action of its outer primary feathers which actually bend the wings forward on the down beat.

He started his gliding experiments in 1891. His first glider had a wing area of about 100 sq. ft. and was built of canvas, willow and bamboo, braced with wire. For take-off he first ran along and jumped off a springboard. Then he used some convenient hills near Berlin, but finally he used an artificial hill at Gross Lichtenfelde, also near Berlin, so that he could run down for a few yards and then sail into the air. The hill, about 50 feet high, and standing in flat country giving steady winds, enabled him to make glides of about 100 yards.

Lilienthal built a number of gliders. Most of them were monoplanes, but one was a biplane with a wingspan of eighteen feet. He controlled them by swinging his legs and shifting the weight of his body. Taking off from the Rhinower Hills, near Stöllen, he made glides of 750 feet.

In 1896, Lilienthal was making plans for powered flight. He would use a two-and-a-half-horsepower

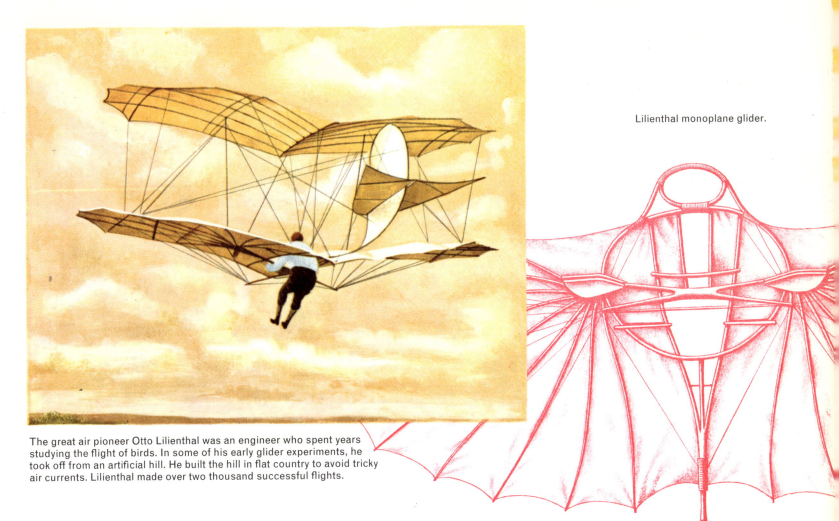

The great air pioneer Otto Lilienthal was an engineer who spent years studying the flight of birds. In some of his early glider experiments, he took off from an artificial hill. He built the hill in flat country to avoid tricky air currents. Lilienthal made over two thousand successful flights.

motor, driven by compressed carbonic acid gas. On August 9, he tested a glider with mechanical steering controls. The glider crashed, and Lilienthal was killed. Just before he died, he said, 'Sacrifices must be made.'

During his lifetime, Lilienthal made more than 2,000 flights. His notes and drawings, and photographs of his flights, were studied by students of flying everywhere. One of the students was Percy Pilcher, a young Englishman. He even visited Lilienthal in Germany to discuss problems of gliding.

Pilcher built four gliders and made many successful flights. Then he, too, began to think of flying with power. He could not find the right type of engine to turn the propeller, so he designed one himself, to be run by oil. The engine was being built when, in 1899, he put on a demonstration of one of his gliders. A wire brace gave way, and Pilcher crashed. He died a few days later.

Another student of Lilienthal's work was Octave Chanute. He was a famous engineer, known throughout the world for his bridges and railroads. Born in France, Chanute had been brought to the United States as a child. He was sixty-four years old when, in 1896, he designed and built his first glider. Because of his age, he made few flights himself. Most of the flying was done by A. M. Herring, who had been Lilienthal's pupil.

Chanute built several kinds of gliders. They included multiplanes, and a biplane which made 700 flights. He also experimented with a new type of controls. The craft were tested on the sand dunes of Indiana, along Lake Michigan.

Once, waiting for a glider to be launched, Chanute suddenly looked upward. His eyes searched the sky, as if he had just heard the engine-roar of an aeroplane over the lake. He stood there pulling at his little white beard, then shook his head slowly and thoughtfully. He was sure that soon there would be planes with motors, but not yet, not yet. All he could hear was the roar of wind, and the cry of the birds riding the restless air.

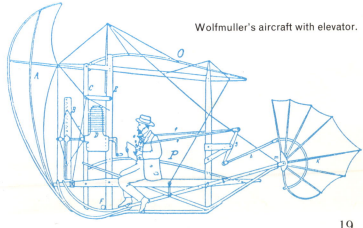

Wolfmuller's aircraft with elevator.

The world's first controlled flight in a powered aircraft.

THE WRIGHTS MAKE HISTORY

The cold north wind came up at night, roaring in to Kitty Hawk from the ocean. It tore spray from the waves crashing on shore and whipped up the sands of the beach.

Inside their hut, the Wright brothers were asleep. Wilbur lay quietly, but Orville kept waking and tossing.

'I am going to fly tomorrow,' he said to himself, again and again. 'I am going to fly tomorrow.'

Then, listening to the wind, he was not so sure. He became a little angry, too. He and Wilbur had come here to make history. Were they to be stopped by the wind?

In the morning, when the brothers got up, the wind was still blowing. They waited for it to die down, and around ten o'clock they decided to wait no longer. They ran up a flag on a pole, signalling the men at the Coast Guard station at Kill Devil Hill. Inspite of the wind,

the Wrights were going to try powered flight, and they needed the men to help.

Glancing up at the flag, they turned and went back into the hut. There they looked carefully at their aircraft, which they called the *Flyer*. It was a biplane, with a four-cylinder petrol engine they had built themselves. The carburettor was an old tomato tin, but the engine was light and powerful, better than anything they could buy.

They pulled the *Flyer* out on the sand, and began laying down two-by-fours to form a long rail. The *Flyer* would be placed on a little truck that had wheels made of bicycle hubs, and would run on the rail for the take-off.

Several times the cold drove the brothers inside the hut, where they warmed themselves at a fire. Just as they were finishing their work on the rail, four men from the Coast Guard station came walking up.

The men helped to put the *Flyer* on the truck, and

The Wrights made four historic flights on December 17, 1903:
120 feet in 12 seconds
195 feet in 11 seconds
over 200 feet in 15 seconds
852 feet in 59 seconds

Wilbur started the engine. The roar of the motor joined the roar of the wind over the dunes. The *Flyer* trembled, as if anxious to be off, but it was held back by a cable.

Orville let the engine warm up for ten minutes. It was twenty-five minutes to eleven when he climbed into the plane. He lay down on the lower wing and put his hands on the controls.

'Ready, Orv?' said Wilbur, shouting over the noise of the engine.

Orville nodded and released the cable. The *Flyer* started to move along the rail, while Wilbur ran with it, steadying the wing. At the end of the rail the plane rose into the air. For a moment it dipped as it fought the wind, and Orville thought he would crash. Then it rose again to a height of about ten feet. It flew, landing safely on the sand 120 feet away.

Orville jumped out of the plane and Wilbur ran toward him. The brothers looked at each other, smiling, too excited to speak. Then they burst out:

'We did it, Orv!'

'We can fly!'

The plane had been in the air only twelve seconds,

but those were twelve seconds of history. As Orville was to write later, it was the first flight 'in which a machine carrying a man raised itself by its own power into the air in full flight; it had sailed forward without reduction of speed, and had finally landed at a point as high as that from which it had started'.

Wooden wind-tunnel used by the Wright brothers for their experiments on various wing sections.

This simple experiment with a spool, a pin, and a piece of cardboard illustrates an important principle of flight: when air flows past a surface, pressure against the surface is lowered. As air is blown through the spool, pressure keeps the disc from falling.

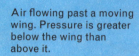

Air flowing past a moving wing. Pressure is greater below the wing than above it.

HOW THE WRIGHTS FLEW

And so at last, after hundreds of years of failure, the aeroplane had been invented by the Wright brothers. But how did their plane fly? What kept it from falling to earth?

The reason had been discovered in 1738 by Daniel Bernoulli, a Swiss mathematician. Scientists already knew that the air has weight, and presses against the surface of anything it touches. Then Bernoulli found that when air flows past a surface, the pressure against the surface is lowered. And the faster the air flows, the less the pressure.

This discovery was later tested in a simple experiment with a spool, a pin, and a disc of light cardboard. The person conducting the experiment stuck the pin through the centre of the disc. He held the disc against the bottom of the spool, with the pin sticking up inside the spool. He blew downward through the spool and took away his hand. Instead of falling, the disc remained in place.

To someone who did not know about air pressure, it might have looked like magic. Actually, by blowing through the spool, the air was made to flow over the top of the disc in all directions. The pressure against the top of the disc was lowered. Meanwhile, the air was pushing up against the bottom of the disc with its usual pressure

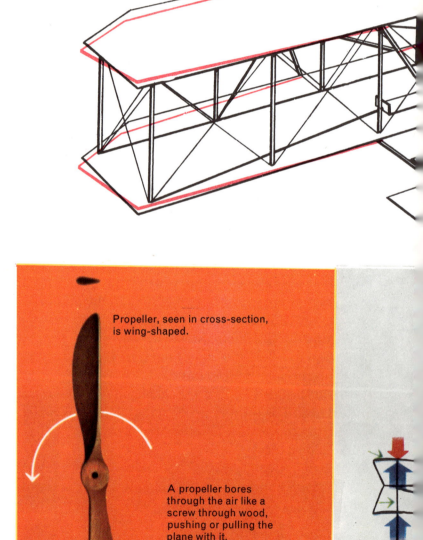

Propeller, seen in cross-section, is wing-shaped.

A propeller bores through the air like a screw through wood, pushing or pulling the plane with it.

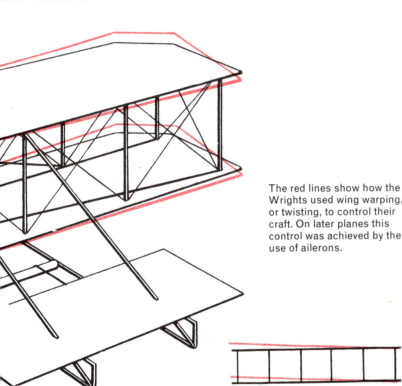

Gliders are carried upward by warm air rising from fields or flowing over hills.

The red lines show how the Wrights used wing warping, or twisting, to control their craft. On later planes this control was achieved by the use of ailerons.

The four forces that work on a plane:

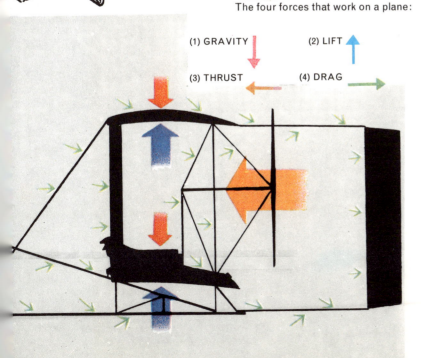

(1) GRAVITY (2) LIFT
(3) THRUST (4) DRAG

—nearly fifteen pounds per square inch. As soon as the person experimenting ran out of breath, the pressure against the top and the bottom of the disc became equal, and gravity made the disc fall.

It was air pressure, too, that kept up the Wrights' plane. They did not know about Bernoulli's discovery, but they experimented with many different shapes of wings. They learnt that a curved wing is best. The air flowing over the top of the wing travels faster than the air flowing underneath it. The air presses harder against the bottom of the wing giving it lift, or upward push.

But, to use air pressure, the wing must be kept moving. This was why the Wrights launched their gliders from a hill. They coasted downward through the air, so the speed was enough to give the wings lift. If the air itself were moving upward at a higher speed, as it does over hills or warm fields, it would carry the glider up with it. In this way the glider could fly higher than the take-off point.

By the time the Wrights decided to try powered flight, they knew that there are four forces which act on any aeroplane. *Lift* keeps it up. *Gravity* tries to pull the plane down. *Drag,* caused by the resistance of the air, tries to hold it back. *Thrust* pulls it forward.

To give their plane thrust, the Wrights used a propeller turned by an engine. It was shaped something like an aeroplane wing, so that the air flowed faster over the front of the blade than over the back. The pressure at the front was less than the pressure at the back. The propeller was drawn forward, carrying the plane with it. Whether the propeller was placed before the wing or behind it made no difference. The Wrights placed their propeller behind the wing, and the plane was pushed through the air, rather than pulled.

There was still one more problem to be solved— controlling the plane. The Wrights had the answer to that, too. In their experiments with gliders, they had discovered something important. They could raise or lower one end of the wing by warping, or twisting, the wing-tip. Warping the wing-tip upward raised that end of the wing. Warping it downward lowered the wing. And the glider always turned in the direction of the lower end.

The Wrights soon found a practical way of warping wings. They ran cables from the wing-tips to levers beside the pilot. To help keep the glider steady during turns, they built rudders at the rear. These could be turned right and left by cables attached to the levers. The Wrights also added an elevator, or small wing, to the front of the glider for climbing and diving.

The Wrights tested this method of control on their glider. They used the same method when they built their first plane, and it worked.

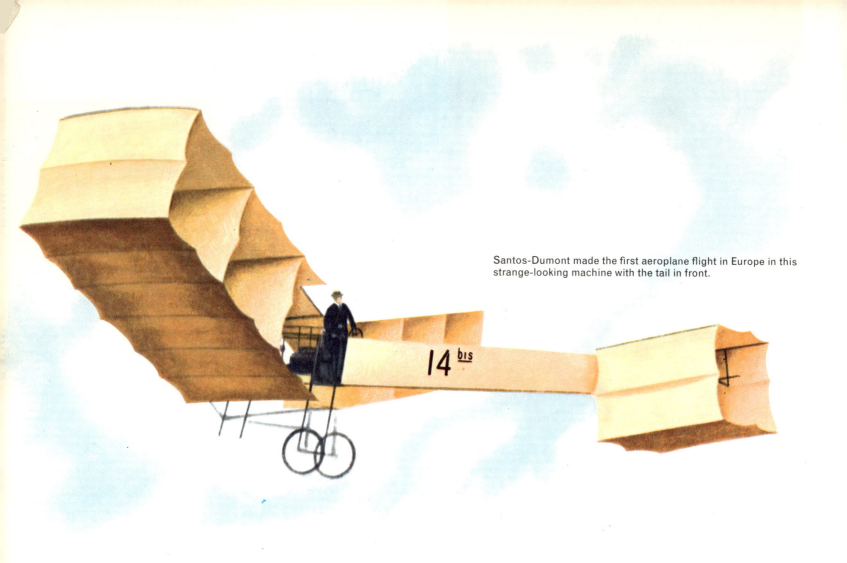

Santos-Dumont made the first aeroplane flight in Europe in this strange-looking machine with the tail in front.

GIFT OF POWERED FLIGHT

Just as they had said in their telegram, the Wright brothers were home in time for Christmas. No crowds met them at the railroad station. There were no cheers, no brass bands. There were no speeches. Only their father, and their sister Katherine, came hurrying up smiling, to shake them warmly by the hand.

On the streets, people walked past, carrying packages,

Karl Jatho's biplane, in which he achieved a hop-flight of nearly 200 feet, in 1903.

wreaths, mistletoe. They scarcely glanced at the Wrights. Few people in the country, let alone in Dayton, believed the Wrights could fly. The newspapers printed little about them. The two brothers had given the world a Christmas gift—the gift of powered flight—and no one realised its significance.

The Wrights were satisfied to have things that way. They were willing enough to let the world know that they could fly. But they had worked hard for many years, and now they wanted to make some money from their invention. They were anxious to keep their method of steering a secret until the aircraft could be patented and sold.

For a while they went on experimenting. They built another aeroplane in 1904, flying it over a 68-acre cow pasture near Dayton. In 1905, they built a third and better plane. On the third of October, they made a record-breaking flight of 24.2 miles in 38 minutes. After that, afraid that their invention might be stolen, they gave up flying for two and a half years.

By this time, the farmers in the neighbourhood were used to seeing the Wright's aeroplane soaring overhead. Passengers on the trolley line that ran by the pasture

24

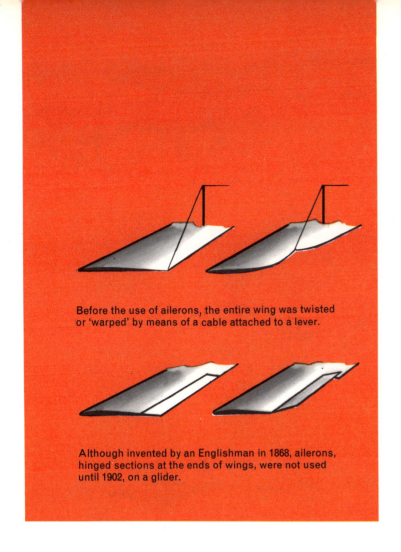

Before the use of ailerons, the entire wing was twisted or 'warped' by means of a cable attached to a lever.

Although invented by an Englishman in 1868, ailerons, hinged sections at the ends of wings, were not used until 1902, on a glider.

The Danish pioneer, Ellerhammer, is reported to have made some short hop flights in this aeroplane in September, 1906.

had often seen it, too. And still, outside Dayton, there were many people who refused to believe the Wrights could fly. Among them were men in the United States government. Three times the Wrights offered to build a practical aeroplane for the army, and three times they were turned down.

But word about the Wrights was slowly spreading, reaching across the sea to Europe. In fact, Europe knew about the Wrights even before they flew their first powered aeroplane. In April, 1903, Octave Chanute visited Paris, where he gave a lecture at the French Aero Club. He told of his own gliders, and of the Wrights'. Several months later he wrote an article on the same subject for a French aviation magazine.

At once, the French began to get busy, building all sorts of gliders. Busiest of all was another set of brothers, Gabriel and Charles Voisin. They became the first manufacturers of aircraft in history.

It was Alberto Santos-Dumont, however, who gave Europe the gift of powered flight. The courageous Brazilian was already world-famous as a balloonist. He made several flights in 1906, and before a cheering crowd he set a world's record of 690 feet in 21.2 seconds.

His aeroplane, built by the Voisin brothers, was a strange looking contraption that seemed to move backward – but it flew.

The following year, 1907, there were more powered flights in the air over France. Léon Delagrange, a sculptor who became a well-known aviator, flew a craft built by the Voisins. It was a biplane, and it showed the way for all the biplanes to come. The Voisins built another aeroplane which was flown by Henri Farman, an Englishman who lived in France. Louis Blériot, who had made a fortune manufacturing headlights for cars, designed and flew a monoplane. It, too, showed the way for aircraft of the future.

Some of the French designers tried a new method of lateral control, different from the Wrights'. Instead of wing-warping, they used ailerons – sections of wings that could be raised or lowered on hinges.

Other new things were tried. In 1907 France seemed full of air-minded men – thinking and tinkering, planning and experimenting, building and flying.

And then came the year 1908.

Louis Blériot's XI, a later model of the famous monoplane he designed in 1907.

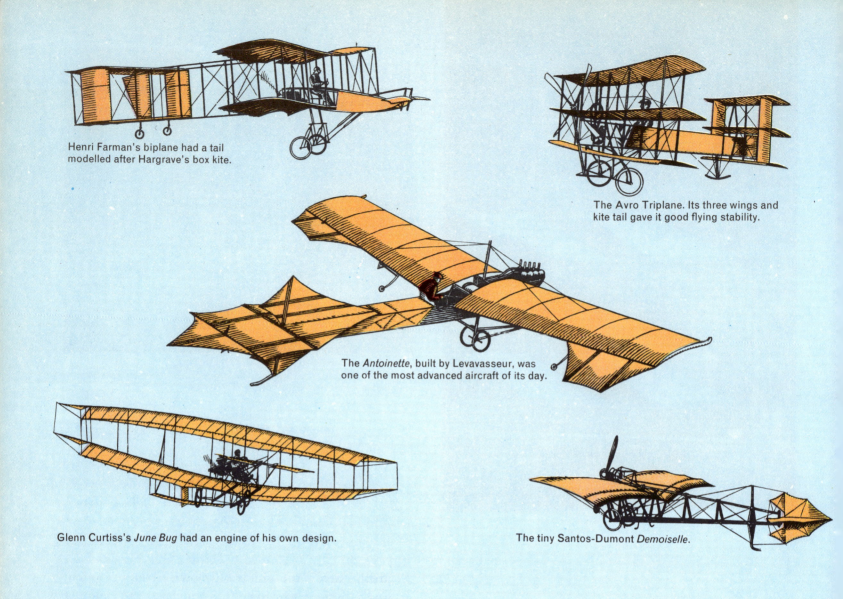

Henri Farman's biplane had a tail modelled after Hargrave's box kite.

The Avro Triplane. Its three wings and kite tail gave it good flying stability.

The *Antoinette*, built by Levavasseur, was one of the most advanced aircraft of its day.

Glenn Curtiss's *June Bug* had an engine of his own design.

The tiny Santos-Dumont *Demoiselle*.

A YEAR TO REMEMBER

On January 13, 1908, Henri Farman won a prize of 50,000 francs for a circular flight of almost one mile. That was the beginning of a great year for aviation, a year to be long remembered.

In France, Léon Levavasseur built the *Antoinette*, a monoplane with many improvements. Farman, Delagrange, and Blériot made longer and longer flights. On one of them Farman stayed in the air for twenty minutes. He also made the world's first cross-country flight, from one town to another, covering about sixteen miles.

In England, too, successful planes were taking to the air. Samuel Franklin Cody, an American who had settled in England after coming there with a Wild West show, flew *British Army Aeroplane No. 1*. Sir Alliott Verdon-Roe built and flew the first of his Avro aircraft.

In the United States, Glenn Curtiss was flying the

planes that would make him famous throughout the world.

And, most important of all, the Wright brothers for the first time demonstrated their *Flyers* in public. The U.S. Army had at last decided to order one of them and set up the Aeronautical Division of the Signal Corps. Meanwhile, on the other side of the ocean, a company was formed to manufacture Wright planes in France.

Up to this time, the Wrights had always flown lying almost flat on their stomachs. Now they arranged the controls so that they could fly in a sitting position, and also have space for a passenger. The brothers practised flying this way at Kitty Hawk, before going separate ways. Orville went to Fort Meyer, near Washington, to demonstrate an aircraft for the army, and Wilbur left for France, to show another of their aircraft at Le Mans. All France buzzed with excitement. Could the Wrights

The historic triplane in which Hans Grade, Germany's first true aviator, made tentative flights in 1908.

1912 Dornier aeroplane.

really fly as well as their own and British pilots? On August 8, a crowd gathered at Le Mans to finally find out.

Wilbur climbed into the *Flyer*. He wore a business suit, with a stiff white collar and tie, as he had at Kitty Hawk. On his head, instead of his usual black derby, was a grey cap. He made a short flight lasting less than two minutes, and the crowd roared. The Wrights could really fly! No doubt about it! And how easily their aircraft handled in the air! Louis Blériot, who was in the crowd, nodded. 'The Wright machine is indeed superior to our aeroplanes,' he said.

While Wilbur flew in France, Orville was getting ready to fly at Fort Myer. On September 3 he made his first flight. The *Flyer* rose and circled the field, and the crowd gasped. When Orville landed, newspaper men rushed toward the plane, tears in their eyes. The crowd, as they reported later, 'went crazy'.

Orville made several more flights that month. On the seventeenth he took up a passenger, Lieutenant Thomas Selfridge of the Signal Corps. One of the propellers split, and the plane crashed from a height of twenty-five feet. Lieutenant Selfridge was killed – the first person

to be killed in an aeroplane accident. Orville was badly injured, and did not fly again for a year.

Wilbur waited until he received word that his brother was recovering, then went on flying. He won prizes, and was awarded gold medals by air clubs in England and France. Famous people – kings and queens, scientists, writers, artists, statesmen – came to meet him. Some of them went on flights as passengers. Every day great crowds thronged to the airfield to see the American fly. And children in the neighbourhood raised their hats to him, smiled and said, 'Bonjour, Monsieur Wright.'

Wilbur was the talk of Europe, but he spoke little himself. Once he said, 'I only know of one bird, the parrot, that talks; and it can't fly very high.'

On December 18 Wilbur reached a record height of 305 feet. Less than two weeks later, on the last day of the year, he broke another record. He remained in the air for 2 hours, 20 minutes, and 23.2 seconds.

That same great year, Sir Hiram Maxim wrote: 'The flying machine has come, and come to stay; and, whether we like it or not, it is a problem that must be taken into serious consideration.'

27

Louis Blériot flew over the white cliffs of Dover after his historic crossing of the English Channel, and landed in a meadow near Dover Castle.

FLIERS MAKE BIG NEWS

In June of 1909, the Wright brothers were back in Dayton. This time the town held a two-day celebration to welcome them. Bells rang, whistles blew, cannon boomed. There were cheering crowds, parades, speeches, brass bands. And only a few days before, the Wrights had been at the White House, where they were honoured by President Taft. At last their own country had accepted the gift of powered flight and was giving its thanks.

Both Wilbur and Orville flew a number of times that year, and began training pilots for the army. But it was not the Wrights who made the big aviation news of 1909.

On the morning of July 25, Louis Blériot stood on a cliff at Calais, France. Below him, almost hidden by the haze, was the English Channel. On the other side of the water, twenty-five miles away, lay England. At four-thirty, Blériot watched the sun come up. Five minutes later he was in the air, trying to fly across the Channel to Dover.

Blériot had no compass to guide him, and in ten minutes he was lost. There was no land anywhere in sight. The sky seemed a vast, empty place, with nothing below it but the rolling sea. And then, after a while, he could make out the cliffs of Dover, and Dover Castle, surrounded by green fields.

But something was happening. The engine was becoming overheated. Listening to its unsteady roar, Blériot looked down at the water. Would there be a ship close enough to pick him up if the aeroplane failed?

Luckily, rain began to fall. It spattered on the aeroplane, cooling the engine. Blériot followed some boats to Dover and circled a green field. He landed in England, thirty-seven minutes after he had left France.

News of the historic aeroplane flight, the first across the Channel, was flashed to the world. Blériot was a hero in Paris and London. But even as the English cheered the brave Frenchman, they felt a touch of fear. No longer could the sea and a mighty navy keep England safe from attack. Enemy aircraft could swoop down on the little island through the open air.

Before a month went by, more big news was flashed to the world. The first international flying meeting began at Rheims, France, on August 22. Huge crowds jammed the town and flocked to the field where the

The Golden Flyer. Designed and built by Glenn Curtiss – the greatest of all the American pioneers after the Wright brothers – this won the Gordon Bennett speed trophy at the famous flying meeting at Rheims in 1909.

meeting was held. They stared, amazed, at the thirty-six aircraft entered in the contests. Five of them were Wrights, although they were not flown by the brothers. Among the other aircraft were eleven Voisins, four Blériots, two Farmans, four *Antoinettes,* four *R.E.P.'s* built by Esnault-Pelterie, two Ariels, one Breguet, one Klutymans, one Fernandez, and one Curtiss.

For a week the meeting went on. Many of the frail aircraft crashed, but no one was killed or seriously hurt. Record after record was broken. Hubert Latham, son of an English father and a French mother, reached an altitude of 508 feet in his *Antoinette.* Henri Farman stayed in the air for 3 hours, 4 minutes, and 56 seconds, to set a new endurance record.

On August 28 came the race for a trophy put up by James Gordon Bennett, publisher of the New York *Herald.* The prize would be given for the fastest two laps around a triangular course of 6.21 miles.

The yelling, excited crowd soon saw that the race would go to one of two men – Glenn Curtiss, the only American in the meet, or Louis Blériot of France. Blériot flew the fastest lap, in 7.47 4/5 minutes, reaching the highest speed yet flown by man. But Curtiss won, with an average speed for the course of 47.65 miles an hour.

As the American flag was raised in his honour, and the band played *The Star-Spangled Banner,* the crowd stood in silence. Then it let out a roar, and people turned to one another, asking: 'Who is this Glenn Curtiss? What has he ever done? Where did this shy young man learn to fly like a demon?'

Glenn Curtiss grew up in Hammondsport, a small town in New York State. He left school when he was

fifteen, but was a born engineer and inventor. He experimented with petrol engines, and then set up a small shop in which to make and sell them. Some of the engines he used himself to help satisfy his one love in life – the love of speed.

Using motorcycles powered by his own engines he won many races. In 1907 he set up a record of 136 miles an hour, for which achievement the newspapers crowned him 'the fastest man on earth'.

One day Dr. Alexander Graham Bell, the inventor of the telephone, visited the Curtiss shop. Dr. Bell explained that he was forming the Aerial Experimental Association – a group of young men to work with him designing and building aeroplanes. Would Curtiss like to join them? 'Yes,' said Curtiss.

The first craft the Association worked on was an incredible multi-celled kite. Although this lifted a man, it had so much drag that it was obviously impractical. The group then built four aircraft.

The third, named the *June Bug,* was designed by Curtiss and was powered by a 40 h.p. lightweight engine of his own design. It was outstandingly successful and on July 4, 1908 won a trophy presented by the magazine *Scientific American* for a flight of nearly a mile. After building a few more aircraft the group broke up.

Curtiss, however, continued to make aircraft, forming America's earliest aircraft manufacturing company with another pioneer, A. M. Herring.

Their first aircraft, the biplane *Gold Bug,* won another *Scientific American* prize in 1909, and was the first aircraft to be sold. The famous *Golden Flyer,* which won the Gordon Bennett trophy at Rheims, was completed only a few weeks before the meeting took place.

Frenchman, Louis Paulhan and his Farman biplane with which he won the *Daily Mail* prize of £10,000 for the first flight from London to Manchester.

THE BIRDMEN

'Then and there every man, woman, and child of the multitude wanted to fly–fly up in the blue, cut away from the earth–fly–fly–oh, the ravishing delight of it!...'

These words were written by a reporter about the first air meeting in America, which took place at Los Angeles in January, 1910. The same story could have been told in France, in England, in Germany, as well as in the United States. For after the great air meeting at Rheims, others were held in many countries.

Record after record was broken. Aircraft flew higher and longer and farther–and that was the ruin of the air meetings. Aircraft were going so high they could not be seen. Aircraft trying for endurance records flew so long that they were tiring to watch. Air meetings soon gave way to long-distance cross-country flights and races. All Europe was shaken by the excitement when birdman Louis Paulhan of France raced against Claude Grahame-White of England. The London newspaper, the *Daily Mail*, had offered a prize of £10,000 in gold for the first flight from London to Manchester to be made in twenty-four hours or less. Paulhan won,

Official Program Friday, Jan. 14 1910

FIRST IN AMERICA
AVIATION MEET
LOS ANGELES
JANUARY 10-20 1910

American & Foreign Aviators
DAILY FLIGHTS

SOUTHERN CALIFORNIA DAY
PRICE 10 CENTS

covering the 183 miles in 5 hours, 15 minutes of flying time.

The following year, 1911, an American set out to cross the United States, from the Atlantic to the Pacific coasts. He was Calbraith Perry Rodgers, grand-newphew of Oliver Hazard Perry, a hero of the War of 1812. Rodgers was well prepared for trouble. Travelling the same route was a special train pulling a carload of spare parts, tools, and fuel. The train also carried three mechanics to work on the aircraft, Rodgers' mother, his wife, his manager, and a chauffeur. The expense of the flight was paid by a company that made Vin Fizz, a soft drink, and the aircraft was named the *Vin Fizz Flyer*.

There were no airports for Rodgers to land on, and he crashed fifteen times. All sorts of things went wrong with the aircraft. By the time he reached California it had been almost completely rebuilt. The flight took forty-nine days for a distance of 4,251 miles. Rodgers made sixty-eight hops, and his average speed was 51.59 miles an hour. A train or motor car would have finished the trip in far better time. But the important thing was that an aeroplane had crossed a continent.

Besides making long flights, aviators went about giving exhibitions of flying at various places, at carnivals and fairs. And everywhere crowds came to watch the stunts of the birdmen, as the aviators were called. In the United States, Glenn Curtiss often gave exhibitions, and the Wrights sent out fliers to show off their aircraft.

Most famous of the American birdmen was Lincoln Beachey. One of his favourite tricks was picking a handkerchief off the ground with a wingtip. In 1911 he amazed the world by flying over the thundering waters of Niagara Falls and diving under the Falls Bridge. Aviators themselves were astonished when, in 1913, Nesterov, a Russian birdman, flew the first 'loop-the-loop'.

At this time women, too, were taking to the air. The first of them was the Baroness Raymonde de LaRoche of France, who started flying in 1909. Two years later, Denise Moore, an American, became the first woman flier to die in an aeroplane accident.

Not that such deaths were unusual. The birdmen flew flimsy craft and had few instruments. But aviation was something new and wonderful, and they could not keep from trying more and more daring stunts. In one year alone, 1910, thirty-two birdmen were killed. Lincoln Beachey said angrily that the crowds that watched him fly came to see his death. If this was true, the crowd at San Francisco in 1915 was satisfied. The wings of his aircraft collapsed in mid-air, and he was killed in the crash.

The birdmen lived to fly. Never was life so sweet as when they were in the air – and never was death so close.

Racing an automobile was a favourite stunt of birdmen. They flew against such famous racing drivers as Barney Oldfield. Sometimes the aircraft won; sometimes it didn't.

Famous stunt flier Lincoln Beachey flew under the bridge at Niagara Falls.

The birdwomen were daring, and their clothes were considered daring too.

31

MIDGET AND GIANT, METAL AND WATER

During the early 1900's, while the birdmen roamed the sky, designers and builders were at work in their shops. A number of interesting aircraft were turned out. One was a midget. Another was a giant. Some, like ducks, could take off from, and come down on water. One was made of metal, and another was built in a church.

The midget was the *Demoiselle*, flown by Santos-Dumont in 1909. It had a wingspan of only eighteen feet and was unusually light. The lever that controlled the wing-warping was behind the pilot's seat. Santos-Dumont attached it to the back of his coat, and worked it by leaning in one direction or another.

Thousands of miles away in California, Glenn Martin was trying out his wings. An automobile dealer, Martin rented an unused church and built his aircraft there in the evenings. His mother held a lantern for him and helped in every way she could. The machine was successful, and within a few years Martin was manufacturing aircraft.

In 1910 John Moisant, a Chicago architect, built an aeroplane of metal instead of wood and cloth. At the same time, in both France and the United States, men were working on aircraft that behaved like ducks.

On a rainy November day, Eugene Ely flew a Curtiss machine from a special sloping deck built on the U.S. Navy cruiser *Birmingham*. At a later date he made a landing on the battleship *Pennsylvania* in San Francisco Bay. The aircraft was equipped with hooks, which caught on ropes stretched from sandbags on either side of the deck.

The first seaplane, with floats for landings and take-offs on the water, was built by a Frenchman, Henri Fabré. A year later, after many failures, Glenn Curtiss successfully tested his first seaplane at California. He soon was an expert on this type of craft and is called the father of naval aviation.

England and Italy, too, began building seaplanes. By 1913 the first Schneider Trophy race for seaplanes was being held at Monaco. This international contest was held twelve times between 1913 and 1931, and helped to produce speedier aircraft and more powerful engines.

The giant aeroplane, one of the first with more than a single engine, was *Le Grand*, built in Russia by Igor Sikorsky. *Le Grand* had four engines of 100 horsepower each, a wing-spread of 92 feet, and weighed 9,000 pounds. The closed cabin had room for eight people, and there was also an outside platform where the passengers could stand. Unlike other planes of that time, the huge biplane carried instruments such as an air-speed indicator, an altimeter, and a bank indicator. Sikorsky's giant showed the way for the airliners of the future, and for the big bombers that would bring terror and death to thousands from the sky.

The first of the famous Schneider Trophy races for seaplanes was won by Maurice Prevost in a 160 h.p. *Deperdussin*, at a speed of 45.75 m.p.h.

The giant four-engine *Le Grand*, built by Igor Sikorsky in Russia in 1913, was the world's largest aeroplane.

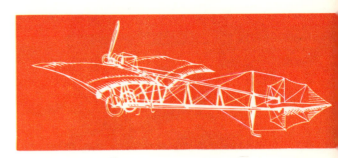

Santos-Dumont's tiny *Demoiselle* had a wing-span of only eighteen feet. Nicknamed 'The Infuriated Grasshopper,' it was a tricky machine to handle. The pilot, who had very little room, sat far forward underneath the wings.

Eugene Ely landing on the deck of a ship.

Ely, a Curtiss pilot, made aviation history twice. Above – taking off from the cruiser *Birmingham*, using a specially-built platform. Left – landing on the battleship *Pennsylvania*. Cables across the deck engaged a hook on the aircraft, dragging it to a halt.

Allied aerial gunner of World War I.

Identification chart published in England in 1915 showed the silhouettes of German and English aircraft. The public was warned to take shelter if enemy aircraft, or airships, were sighted. One year later the Germans bombed London.

WAR IN THE AIR

In 1670, Father Francesco de Lana looked into the bright Italian sky and dreamed of airships. He saw that they could make war and bring down death upon the earth, and wrote that 'God would surely never allow such a machine to be successful, since it would cause much disturbance among the governments of mankind'.

And in 1903, when the Wrights flew above the sands of Kitty Hawk, they thought the aeroplane was such a terrible weapon that it would make war impossible.

Then, in 1914, World War I began in Europe, and the aeroplane turned the sky into a field of battle.

It was not the first time aircraft had been used in war. Balloons had been used for scouting the enemy in the Civil War in America, and to carry messages and men in the Franco-Prussian War. In World War I, the Germans tried something new—bombing cities from zeppelins. The giant airships were too easy to attack and most of them were destroyed.

Later, both the Germans and the Allies dropped

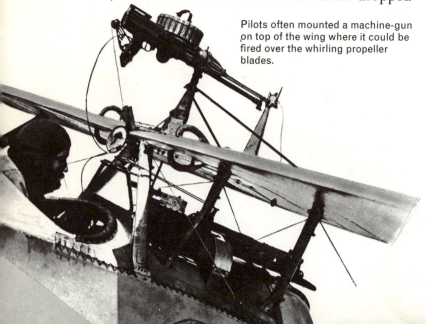

Pilots often mounted a machine-gun on top of the wing where it could be fired over the whirling propeller blades.

bombs from aircraft. But at the start of the war, the job of aircraft was still scouting and observation of ground troops. A German army report in 1914 said, 'The duty of the aviator is to see, and not to fight.' Few generals in any army would have disagreed.

And so, when enemy fliers passed each other in the air, they waved their hands in greeting. But one day an English pilot took a shot at a German with a shotgun. Soon fliers of both sides were firing at each other with revolvers, rifles, and, finally, machine guns. Some two-seater aircraft carried a gunner as well as a pilot.

Then Roland Garros, a noted French pilot, fired a machine gun right through his whirling propeller blades. He had placed metal plates on the back of the blades. About one out of every fifteen bullets fired hit the metal plates and glanced off. The rest of the bullets missed the propeller and sped toward the enemy. Using this amazing device, Garros brought down five German aircraft in eighteen days.

In April of 1915, Garros was forced to land in German territory. His aircraft was studied by Anthony Fokker, a Dutch aeronautical designer working for Germany. He quickly turned out a better device than Garros', hooking up the machine-gun trigger to the engine. The gun was timed to fire only when the propeller blades were out of the way. Fokker's device gave the Germans control of the air until the Allies developed a hydraulically operated interrupter gear which also timed the bullets to miss the propeller blades, but permitted a more rapid rate of fire.

Generals no longer tried to keep fliers from fighting, but asked their governments for more aircraft and pilots. The aeroplane had become a weapon of war.

A 'dog-fight' of World War I, with the German ace Von Richthofen in his red Fokker triplane. In the foreground is the aircraft of the American ace, Eddie Rickenbacker. In real life the two airmen never met; Von Richthofen was shot down before Rickenbacker had begun to fly in combat.

Pilots in World War I, who at first did their fighting in single combat, developed many daring manoeuvres to use against the enemy. Aeroplanes were still crude, and it took great skill to handle them.

KNIGHTS OF THE SKY

Like the knights of a time long past, the fliers of World War I at first fought in single combat. It was man against man, 'plane against plane'. Some fliers became aces—airmen who had shot down five or more enemy aircraft. The most famous ace was Baron Manfred von Richthofen of Germany, with 80 victories. Then came René Fonck of France with 75 victories, Edward Mannock of England with 73, and William Bishop of Canada with 72.

The chance of escaping death was so small that the fliers had to learn to live with fear. Somehow they could

Baron von Richthofen joined the German flying service in 1915. As a challenge to the enemy he painted his plane red, and was known as the Red Knight. In 1917 he began using mass formations, and his fliers were called 'Richthofen's Flying Circus'. He was twenty-five when he was killed in 1918, a day after gaining his eightieth victory.

forget that their flimsy machines might give way, or that they might be shot down in flames. But they could not forget their fear of fear itself. If they had to die, they wanted to die bravely and well.

They found this hard to explain to anyone who had never been in an aircraft. Only another flier would understand the terror of battle in the sky—or the joy and freedom of flight. And so they felt a kind of brotherhood with all fliers, even with the enemy.

It was a strange feeling to have in the midst of war. As the writer James Norman Hall, himself a pilot, said, 'How is an airman, who has just learned a new meaning for the joy of life, to reconcile himself to the insane business of killing a fellow aviator who may have just learned it too?'

And yet, it was their duty to kill, and they could not refuse to do their duty. But, again like the knights of old, they respected the enemy and honoured him for his bravery. Once a German aerial patrol, raiding an air base in France, shot down an American flier. The day of his funeral, the same patrol returned with white streamers attached to their wings, and dropped flowers

Combat manoeuvres were more than aerial acrobatics. They allowed pilots to reverse direction quickly, or to fly above or below enemy aircraft, putting them in better positions to fight or escape.

on the cemetery. And when Von Richthofen was shot down behind Allied lines in the last year of the war, he was buried by the British with full military honours. The next day a British pilot flew over Von Richthofen's squadron air base. He dropped an announcement of the great ace's death and a photograph of Allied pilots firing a last salute over the grave.

Even before the United States entered the war, American volunteers were flying with the Lafayette Escadrille, a famous French squadron. After the United States declared war in 1917, they became a part of the Air Service of their own country. At the same time, the Air Service turned down a racing car driver named Edward Vernon Rickenbacker. He was told he was too old for flying, and did not have the right background and experience. Rickenbacker joined the infantry, served as General Pershing's chauffeur, then managed to get himself transferred to the Air Service. In only eight months of combat flying he scored twenty-five victories and became America's top ace.

Now a captain, Rickenbacker was made flight commander of the 94th Pursuit Squadron. The 94th's emblem was Uncle Sam's hat in a ring, and it was known as the 'Hat-in-the-Ring' Squadron. Captain Rickenbacker probably could have doubled his score of victories, but he was more interested in training his men to work as a team. For pilots no longer roamed the sky like knights, challenging each other to duels. Instead, they flew in formation and fought as a group. War in the air was changing, as airmen tried to find better ways of protecting themselves—and better ways of destroying the enemy.

Edward Mannock, top scoring English ace of World War I. He scored 73 victories.

AIRCRAFT OF WORLD WAR I

When World War I started, Germany had the biggest air force, totalling some 260 aircraft, and probably the best, as many of the aircraft were powered by the efficient and reliable Mercedes engines. France went to war with 156 aeroplanes and Britain mustered 154 of all types. The United States had less than 100.

The armies of the nations at war called for more and better aircraft, and they got them. Behind the lines, designers and builders turned out swift fighter scouts, heavy bombers, and even seaplanes and flying boats for war at sea. Fokker designed a number of fighters for Germany. France had the *Spad*, and Great Britain the Sopwith *Camel*. Among the most famous bombers were the Gothas built in Germany, the DH-4 built in England, and the Italian Caproni.

American aircraft production was disappointing. The only American-built combat 'planes to be delivered were DH-4's. They were based on a British design by Geoffrey de Havilland, and were powered by American-designed Liberty engines. American fliers flew *Spads*, Sopwith *Camels* or other European aircraft. But the United States did produce several thousand Curtiss *Jennies*, which were used for training, and by the time the war ended the country was ready for the mass production of various types of military aircraft.

In May, 1918, while fighters were battling in the air over Europe, the United States began a scheduled air mail service. Army aircraft flew mail between Washington, D.C., and New York City, by way of Philadelphia. After a few months, the Post Office Department was given full charge of air mail.

During World War I, aviation took a tremendous step forward. Governments poured out money to build up their air forces, and inventors and designers were given the help they could never get in times of peace. Then, in 1918, the war ended. One designer said, 'I realised that this great opportunity was gone forever. I should not say I was bitterly disappointed, because we all wanted the war to end, but the truth of the matter is that it was a terrible blow.'

Allied aircraft shown under the American, French, and British insignia; at far right, German aircraft under the German insignia. At the beginning of the war, aircraft carried no identification and were sometimes shot at by their own soldiers. Flags were then painted on the wings. When this proved to be too difficult a job, the Allies worked out simple designs. The Germans followed their example, basing their insignia on the Iron Cross, a famous military decoration.

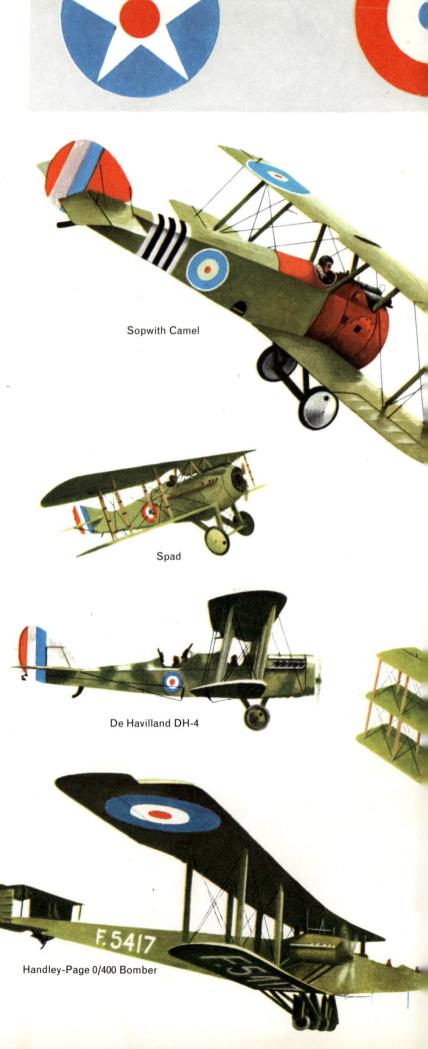

Sopwith Camel

Spad

De Havilland DH-4

Handley-Page 0/400 Bomber

S.E.5a

Curtiss JN-4 Jenny

Caproni Bomber

Albatros DIII Scout

Fokker Eindecker IV

Fokker D.VII

Gotha G IV Bomber

Alcock and Brown's Atlantic flight ended in an Irish bog.

Sixty Army planes took part in a coast-to-coast race across the United States.

The U.S. Navy seaplane NC-4 made the first flight across the Atlantic. The trip from Newfoundland to England was made in several hops, with stops at the Azores and Lisbon.

OVER SEA, OVER LAND

In 1919 the aeroplane was a fact. Men no longer had to dream of flight, or envy the swift movements of birds. Still, they were not satisfied. They wanted to outdo the birds. They wanted to fly farther and faster, over sea as well as over land. Most of all, they wanted to prove that the aeroplane was a good, safe, practical way of travel.

To stimulate interest in aviation, the London newspaper the *Daily Mail* offered a prize of £10,000 for the first non-stop flight across the Atlantic Ocean. Airmen had been thinking of such a flight for some time; now they were ready to try it.

In the United States, the navy began preparing for its attack on the Atlantic. Officials decided against a non-stop flight. Instead, the flight would be made in three hops—from Newfoundland to the Azores; from the Azores to Lisbon, Portugal; and then on to Plymouth, England. Navy pilots would fly NC's, the huge flying boats completed by Curtiss during the last days of the war. Only four were ever built, and one of these was

taken apart to provide parts for the remaining three.

Everything was carefully planned. Sixty-eight destroyers were stationed fifty miles apart along the route to guide the fliers. Five battleships were to take weather observations and report them by radio.

On the evening of May 16, 1919, the three seaplanes took off. Two of the planes became lost in the fog and had to come down at sea. One sank after its five-man crew had been rescued by a freighter. The other stayed afloat and taxied more than 200 miles to the Azores. The third plane, the NC-4, went roaring on to the Azores, to Portugal, and finally to Plymouth. It landed on May 31. Lieutenant Commander Read and his pilots, Lieutenants Hinton and Stone, had covered 3,936 nautical miles in 52 hours, 31 minutes of flying time.

On June 14, another British aircraft also took off from Newfoundland. It was a Vickers Vimy biplane, a heavy bomber type, and its crew were Captain John Alcock and Lieutenant Arthur Whitten-Brown. Over

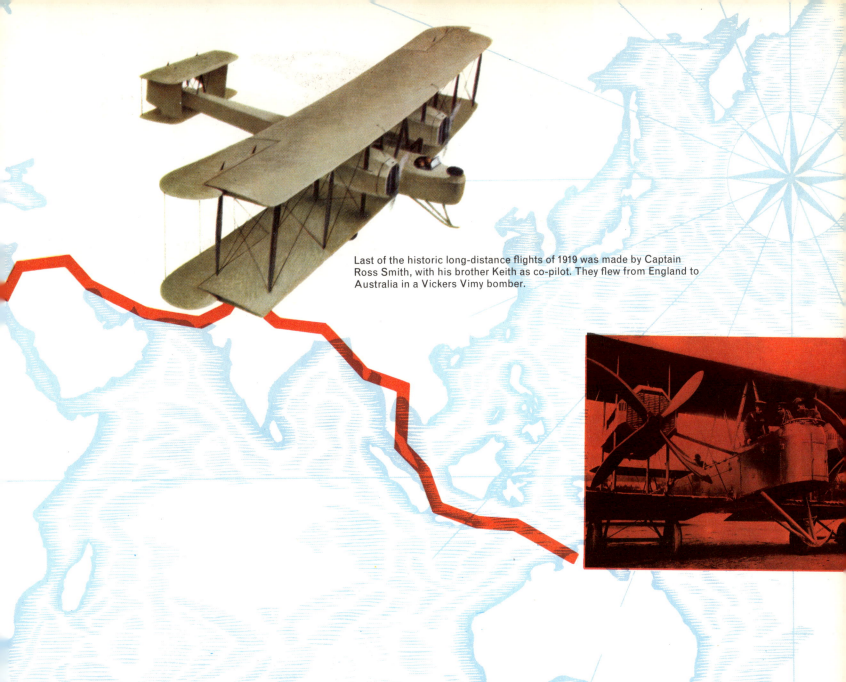

Last of the historic long-distance flights of 1919 was made by Captain Ross Smith, with his brother Keith as co-pilot. They flew from England to Australia in a Vickers Vimy bomber.

the waters of the Atlantic fog, snow, and sleet came swirling at them. Their radio went dead. Several times Brown had to crawl out on the fuselage to remove ice and snow from a petrol gauge. Once the aircraft went into a tailspin and almost fell into the sea.

Around eight o'clock the next morning, the two fliers sighted the coast of Ireland. After landing nose-down in a bog, they climbed out, shaken but safe. So were their passengers—a dog and a cat—and the four-pound sack of mail they carried. It was 15 hours and 57 minutes since they had left Newfoundland, 1,890 miles away. They had made the first non-stop flight over the Atlantic.

Two other contestants challenging the Atlantic included Harry Hawker, with a Sopwith biplane specially built for the competition and appropriately named the *Atlantic*, and his friend Freddie Raynham, with a Martinsyde biplane. The two Englishmen had been ready for some weeks, but the weather had been unfavourable. When the Curtiss flyingboat reached the Azores, however, Hawker and Raynham knew that they just had to leave immediately if they were to have any chance of reaching England first.

And so, on 18 May, the heavily laden *Atlantic* took off and headed out over the coast. For the first few hours all went well, but then the engine began to overheat, and Hawker had to ditch in the sea. He landed close to a ship, and was picked up, wet, but unhurt.

Nor had Raynham fared any better. Trying to take-off shortly after Hawker, a gust of wind caused the little biplane to crash, fortunately without killing its occupants.

The following month, two Australian brothers, Captains Ross and Keith Smith, made a record-breaking 11,000 mile flight from England to Australia. Accompanied by only two mechanics, they took off from Hounslow in a Vickers Vimy bomber on November 12, landing in Darwin on December 10. It was one more proof that men had completely out-done the birds and were the absolute rulers of the air.

In 1924 pioneer Ezra Meeker flew swiftly in sixteen hours over the trail he had taken six months to cross in a covered wagon in 1851.

THE BIG PUSH

Ezra Meeker leaned forward and peered through the window of the aircraft. His old man's hands—he was ninety-four—trembled from the vibration as he touched his long, white beard. For a moment he listened to the roar of the motor, then he looked down at the land below.

He remembered another journey he had taken, seventy-three years ago. And, remembering, he seemed to hear the crack of the oxcart he had driven along the Oregon Trail, westward from Omaha. That was in 1851, and it had taken him six months to reach the State of Oregon. Now, in 1924, he was flying eastward over the same trail, and the trip would take fifteen hours. Shaking his head in wonder, he listened again to the motor. Its roar was like the rush of time moving into the future.

Aviation, too, was moving into the future, a future of airlines, airports and aeroplanes winging their way to the cities of the world. But in the 1920's the men of aviation were impatient. They wanted to hurry time along,

One of the Army DH-4's which flew to Alaska in 1920.

to push on to the days when flying would be a part of everyday life.

The big push began in July, 1920. The U.S. Army Air Service flew four DH-4's from Mitchell Field, Long Island, to Nome, Alaska. The planes returned to New York in October, having covered 4,345 miles in 56 hours of flying time.

As more and more flights were made, record after record was broken. By 1922 the speed record was 236.6 miles per hour. The altitude record was 34,563 feet—more than six and a half miles. In September of that same year, Lieutenant James H. Doolittle flew across America in less than one day. He left Jacksonville, Florida, before dawn, stopped to refuel and have breakfast at San Antonio, Texas, and reached San Diego, California, 21 hours and 20 minutes later.

At San Diego were two other army fliers, Lieutenants John Macready and Oakley Kelly. In October they tried to fly non-stop to New York, but were stopped by fog over the mountains. They tried again in November, and engine trouble forced them down in Indianapolis. In May of 1923 they tried for a third time, taking off from New York in a Fokker T-2 monoplane. They carried a load of 3,000 pounds, and had to fly twenty miles before they could climb above 400 feet. They were too heavy to clear the ridges of the western mountains, and had to fly through the passes. But after 26 hours and 50 minutes they landed in California.

They received a telegram of congratulations from Ezra Meeker, saying, 'Ready to go with you next time'. And the following year Lieutenant Kelly flew the old pioneer to an air meeting at Dayton, Ohio.

Meanwhile, in 1923, Lieutenants Lowell Smith and J. P. Richter stayed aloft thirty-seven hours by refuelling from another aircraft in mid-air. A year later, Lieutenant Russell A. Maughan raced the sun across

the United States in a 'dawn-dusk' flight. Taking off from New York at four o'clock in the morning, he set his course for the West Coast and arrived in San Francisco at sunset. Even with three stops on the way, he travelled 2,540 miles in 17 hours and 52 minutes.

In 1924, too, came the most ambitious flight yet attempted – a trip around the world. It began on April 6, when airmen of the U.S. Army took off from Seattle. They flew four open-cockpit aircraft, single-engine Douglas World Cruisers specially built for this flight. Two of the aircraft were lost, one in Alaska and the other in the Atlantic Ocean, but the crews were rescued.

The other two aircraft went on. They sped over Arctic wastelands, over jungles and deserts and stormy seas, landing in ancient cities of Asia and the great capitals of Europe. Then they returned to the United States. After stopping at Boston, New York, and Washington, they were in Seattle again on September 28. Their flying time was 15 days, 11 hours, and 7 minutes.

And in 1926 Lieutenant Commander Richard E. Byrd of the U.S. Navy and his pilot, Floyd Bennett, set out from Spitsbergen in a Fokker trimotor monoplane. On the morning of May 9 they flew over the North Pole. They returned to Spitsbergen the same day, taking less than 16 hours for the 1,600-mile trip.

The airmen were pushing on into the future, and the roar of their aircraft was like the rush of time.

Army pilots, refuelling in mid-air, made a record-breaking endurance flight in 1923.

U.S. Army planes on their history-making round-the-world flight in 1924. Their flying time for the trip was less than sixteen days.

French airmen Nungesser and Coli fell to their death in the Atlantic.

The Wright Whirlwind engine.

Charles Lindbergh before taking off from Roosevelt Field, New York.

THE RACE TO PARIS

It was in 1919 that Raymond Orteig, a wealthy hotel owner, offered $25,000 for the first non-stop flight between New York and Paris. No pilot dared to try for the prize. For one thing, aeroplane motors were not dependable enough for such a long hop. Seven years passed and better motors were developed, especially the Wright Whirlwind. Built by the Wright Aeronautical Corporation, it was a radial air-cooled engine of 200 horsepower. Suddenly, in 1926, the race to reach the two great cities was on—and for some of the contestants it ended in death.

First to attempt the flight was the great French ace, René Fonck. In September he took off from Roosevelt Field in Long Island, near New York City, with a crew of three. The plane, a Sikorsky, crashed at the end of the runway and two of the crew were killed. In April of 1927, two American naval officers were killed while testing their plane in Virginia.

That same month, Commander Richard E. Byrd was also testing an aircraft for the flight across the ocean. His big trimotor craft was designed by Anthony Fokker, who was now building aircraft in the United States. Fokker himself was in the crew, together with Floyd Bennett and a radioman. Landing in New Jersey, the machine hit a soft spot on the field and nosed over. Bennett and the radioman were injured seriously enough to be taken to a hospital, and Byrd's wrist was broken.

On the other side of the Atlantic, two French airmen, Captains Charles Nungesser and François Coli, were preparing to fly across the ocean from east to west. Because of the prevailing winds, this would be much more difficult than the west-east crossing. On May 8, 1927, they took off from Paris in their plane, the *White Bird,* and the world waited in suspense to hear the news of their landing in New York. Tragically the news never came. Somewhere over the Atlantic the *White Bird* went down, carrying Nungesser and Coli to their death. The cause of the accident was never discovered.

But the race between New York and Paris was still on. At Roosevelt Field, Commander Byrd watched the weather reports and kept his big Fokker ready. At the same field, Clarence Chamberlain and Bert Acosta tinkered with their Bellanca monoplane. Testing it on May 14, they set a new circling endurance record of fifty-one hours in the air, to the amazement of everyone. And on the dark, drizzly morning of May 20, a third aircraft was on the runway at Roosevelt Field. It was the *Spirit of St. Louis,* and the pilot was a slim young man named Charles A. Lindbergh.

From the moment he had first seen an aeroplane, at the age of ten, Lindbergh knew that the only thing he wanted to do was to fly. In 1922 he took his first flying lessons, and in no time at all became a barnstormer. By 1926 he was making a living as an airmail pilot. One night, while flying over the Illinois farmland, he began thinking about making the long hop to Paris. The more he thought about it, the more excited he became with the idea. Of course, he would need an aircraft – a new, improved machine – but what type? Finally, after a lot of thought, he decided on a small, single-engine monoplane. For one thing it would be more efficient than a biplane, and its single engine, while not so safe as three, would allow him to go farther on less fuel. And having sufficient fuel was quite the most important thing, if he wanted to land safely in Europe. To save weight, he made up his mind to fly alone, without a crew. Instead of the extra men, he would carry more fuel.

In March of 1927, Lindbergh was in California, where the Ryan Company was building his aircraft. A group of eight businessmen from St. Louis had furnished the money. Waiting for the machine to be completed, Lindbergh planned his flight, studying all sorts of maps and charts. Then he flew his plane to New York, making one stop at St. Louis, and setting a cross-country speed record.

The weather had been bad, but on the evening of May 19 Lindbergh received a report that the fog over the North Atlantic might be clearing. Early the next morning he was at Roosevelt Field, ready to fly. He carried no radio, no parachute, no sextant. He had thrown away parts of charts he would not need and torn out blank pages from his notebook – all to save weight. To feed the engine, he had 2,750 pounds of fuel. For himself, he had five ham and chicken sandwiches, five cans of army emergency rations, and five quarts of water.

As he slipped on his flying clothes, a thin mist-like rain began to fall. Airfield officials asked him to wait until the weather cleared a little, but Lindbergh shook his head. He climbed into the cockpit and, at exactly 7.54, he took off. Slowly the overloaded machine rolled across the field. It bumped twice and then rose shakily, growing smaller and smaller, until it disappeared into the dark, forbidding sky.

Early on the morning of May 20, 1927, the *Spirit of St. Louis* took off into the fog and rain. Young Charles Lindbergh was attempting what no one had ever dared before – a non-stop, solo flight across the Atlantic.

Charles A. Lindbergh.

THE LONE EAGLE

Sleep was his enemy—sleep and fog and the black storm clouds that came boiling up over the Atlantic. His eyes closed. In less than a minute a sudden dip of the plane brought him awake again. Instantly, his hand tightened on the stick and he levelled off.

'We almost did it that time,' he said.

He no longer thought of himself as Charles A. Lindbergh, flying the *Spirit of St. Louis*. He and the 'plane were one. They belonged to each other, and he thought of himself and the aircraft as 'we'. Together they hung in an ocean of air above an ocean of water, in the lonely space between two continents. Together they would reach land again, or together they would fail.

At the beginning of the flight, between Cape Cod and Nova Scotia, the weather had cleared. From Nova Scotia to Newfoundland the sea was caked with ice, but as he drew near the coast there was no ice, and he saw ships on the water. Then, instead of ships, there were icebergs, one after another. Evening came, and darkness. With the darkness came a thin fog, through which the icebergs loomed like pale, wandering ghosts. The fog thickened and storm clouds surrounded him. He flew over and around the clouds, making his way through the darkness.

After the moon rose, the flying was easier. It was easier still after sunrise. He dropped through a hole in the fog until he could see the white-capped waves. The fog kept clearing, then coming back again. Often he flew blind, using instruments.

But sleep was the real enemy. He fought back, trying to hold an eyelid open with his thumb. He took a sip of water. He shifted in his seat. But he kept dozing off and waking again with a start. Ten hours passed, fifteen, eighteen, twenty, twenty-one, twenty-two, twenty-three. The fog broke up into shreds and patches that took on the shapes of dreams—phantoms, weird animals, monsters. Then he saw the shoreline of islands against the horizon. If he had not known he was in the

Instrument panel of the *Spirit of St. Louis*.

46

Lindbergh's plane over the lights of Paris after his crossing of the Atlantic.

hours, watching the sky. They swarmed around him, pushing aside the policemen who tried to hold them back. They pulled him out of the cockpit and hoisted him on to their shoulders. No longer did he belong to the aircraft. He belonged to the crowd now, and to the world. Other men had flown the Atlantic, but none had flown alone, in so small an aircraft—and the world needed a hero.

Later, in Belgium and England, as well as in France, Lindbergh was surrounded by cheering crowds. Government officials greeted him. The United States sent a naval cruiser to take him and his aircraft home. In Washington, President Coolidge made a speech and awarded him the Distinguished Flying Cross. In New York and St. Louis, crowds gave him a wild welcome. Everywhere newspapers carried stories about him. Plucky Lindy, Lucky Lindy, they called him, and the Lone Eagle.

Everywhere people talked about Lindbergh, and about aviation. He had done more than fly across the ocean. He had awakened the world to the fact that it had entered a new age—the age of flight.

New Yorkers gave 'Lindy' a hero's welcome after his historic flight.

middle of the Atlantic, he would have believed they were real.

He dozed, wakened, dozed, wakened. He seemed to hear voices calling to him from somewhere. But as the fog cleared, his head cleared, too. He flew lower, sometimes almost skimming the waves. He saw birds, porpoises and, at last, some fishing boats. On one of the boats a man stared from the cabin window. Circling the boat, Lindbergh shouted, 'Which way is Ireland?'

There was no answer, so he flew on. The hours were going faster now. He sighted the hazy coast of Ireland, saw ships on the sea. He passed over England, with its neatly laid-out farms, and over the Channel to France. After sunset he followed the beacons of the London-Paris airway, and then saw the lights of Paris itself. He circled the Eiffel Tower and found the lights of Le Bourget, the flying field. The roads leading to the field were crowded with cars. He circled the field, heading into the wind, and brought the aircraft down for the landing.

The flight was over. He had covered 3,600 miles in 33 hours and 31 minutes, and his machine still held eighty-five gallons of fuel.

As soon as the aircraft touched ground, thousands of people came running toward him. They had waited for

Kingsford-Smith flew the Pacific to Australia.

Wiley Post's famous round-the-world aeroplane.

Crew of the first plane to fly the Atlantic from east to west.

Lieutenant Doolittle made the first 'blind' flight.

Amelia Earhart's Lockheed Electra.

Amelia Earhart, the most famous woman pilot of her day, made many record-breaking flights.

Commander Byrd (second from left) and the men who flew the Atlantic with him.

THE RECORD BREAKERS

And still the flights went on, over land and over sea. Any records that had ever been made could be broken, and there were men—and women, too—who longed to break them.

On June 4, 1927, two weeks after Lindbergh's flight, Clarence Chamberlain flew non-stop from New York to Germany, covering 3,911 miles in 42 hours and 45 minutes. Altogether, within a year of Lindbergh's flight, there were ten crossings of the Atlantic. Twenty-one other attempts were unsuccessful, and twenty men and women lost their lives.

And still the flights went on and records were broken. In 1928, Captain James Fitzmaurice of the Irish Free State and Baron Guenther von Huenefeld and Captain Herman Koehl of Germany, made the first non-stop

east-west crossing of the Atlantic. And in 1930 two Frenchmen, Dieudonné Coste and Maurice Bellonte, flew non-stop from Paris to New York.

With the Atlantic conquered, fliers turned to the Pacific. On June 28, 1927, Lieutenants Lester J. Maitland and Albert F. Hegenberger of the U.S. Army took off from Oakland, California. They landed in Honolulu after flying 2,400 miles in 25 hours and 50 minutes. In May of 1928 Captains Charles Kingsford-Smith and Charles Ulm of Australia, with two Americans as navigator and radio operator, also flew from California to Honolulu. Then they made another hop of 4,762 miles to Brisbane, Australia.

All sorts of flights were made during the 1920's and 1930's. On November 28, 1929, Commander Byrd, who with Floyd Bennett had flown to the North Pole three years before, made the first trip over the South Pole. He and his crew of three flew a Ford trimotor. That same year, Lieutenant James Doolittle made a short but important flight, the first 'blind' flight in history. Using only radio beams and instruments, he took off, flew for fifteen miles, and landed without being able to see outside the cockpit.

In Britain the appearance of the de Havilland *Moth* in 1925 led to a series of record breaking and long distance flights by this popular little single-engined biplane. In May, 1925, Sir Alan Cobham flew a *Moth* a thousand miles from Croydon to Zurich and back, in a day. In 1927 Lieutenant Bentley made two return trips from Croydon to Cape Town, and in Australia in 1928 a *Moth* broke the Perth to Melbourne record.

A *Moth* was used by Amy Johnson for her famous first England to Australia solo flight by a woman in 1930. A *Moth* was also used for a solo flight over this route by Francis Chichester, who thirty years later reaped further fame by sailing round the world single-handed.

Italy's General Italo Balbo led a mass flight to Rio de Janeiro in January, 1931. In June, Wiley Post and Harold Gatty flew a Lockheed monoplane around the world in 8 days, 15 hours, and 51 minutes. Two years later, flying alone, Post broke his own record by making the same trip in 7 days, 8 hours, and $49\frac{1}{2}$ minutes.

In 1928 Amelia Earhart became the first woman to

Clarence Chamberlain and Charles Levine made the first non-stop flight to Germany in this Bellanca monoplane.

cross the Atlantic by air, flying as a passenger in an aircraft piloted by William Stultz. In 1932, like Lindbergh, she flew the ocean alone. Bad weather and instrument failure forced her machine down in Ireland, but her time from Newfoundland was 13 hours, 30 minutes, setting a new record.

Known as 'The Lady Lindbergh', she made many more flights and broke many records. In 1937 she and her navigator, Fred Noonan, set out on a flight around the world. While flying over the Pacific, from New Guinea to Howland Island, she broadcast a radio message. She said that she was out of sight of land, that she was running out of fuel, and was lost. 'Position doubtful', the message said—and those were the last words ever heard from her. The world waited anxiously while ships and planes searched the wide waters of the Pacific, but Amelia Earhart was gone.

Commander Richard E. Byrd became the first man to conquer both poles by air when he flew over the South Pole in 1929. His plane, a Ford Trimotor, was piloted by the noted Arctic flier, Bernt Balchen.

The DC-3 gave the airlines the practical aircraft they needed to develop air transport throughout the world.

WANTED—A PRACTICAL AIRLINER

Air transport—carrying passengers and freight in aircraft—was begun by the British, who organised Aircraft Transport and Travel Ltd. for military use during World War I. In 1919 the company began regular flights between London and Paris. European governments were quick to see the importance of commercial aviation and aided their airlines with government money. By the 1920's many countries in Europe, including Britain, France, Belgium, Holland, Denmark, and Germany, had regular airline services to distant places.

The first American airline was Aeromarine Airways Inc., with flights between Key West, Florida, and Havana, Cuba. It began operating in 1921, but was out of business by 1923. The United States did better with airmail service, which had the support of the government, than it did with commercial airlines. In 1924 aircraft were flying mail by night along an airway marked by gas and electric beacons, with emergency landing fields every twenty-five or thirty miles.

The real start of American airlines came in 1926, when Congress passed the Kelly bill. This bill allowed the Post Office to turn over air mail routes to private companies. Carrying mail was profitable and kept the companies in business. They began to carry passengers, too, and over the years built up a network of air travel.

But in the 1920's the development of both American and European airlines was held back by the aircraft themselves. One of the most popular craft was the Fokker trimotor transport, whose wings and fuselage were covered with plywood. It was a good machine, but it could carry only eight passengers and reach a speed of 100 miles an hour. Besides, its construction made it hard to inspect. And after Knute Rockne, a famous football coach, was killed in the crash of a Fokker, people felt that aircraft of this type were not safe. Most flying was still done in craft made of wood covered with fabric.

What the airlines needed was a practical aeroplane—a faster, safer, more comfortable craft—that could be operated cheaply enough to make money. The answer seemed to be an aircraft made entirely of metal. The United States already had such a machine, the Ford *Tri-Motor*, designed by William Bushnell Stout and manufactured by Henry Ford. It became widely known as a sturdy, dependable craft, and airmen fondly called

50

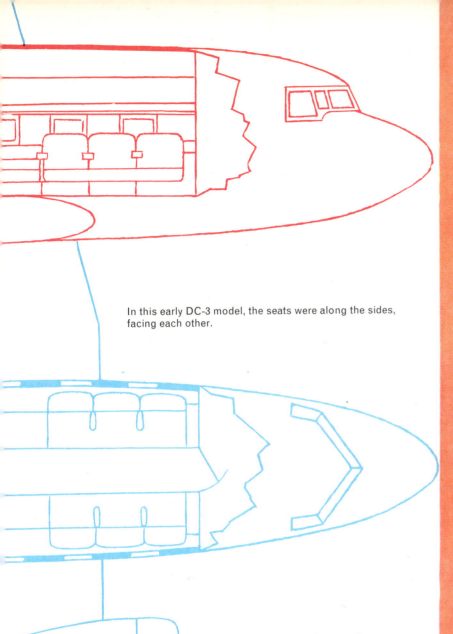

In this early DC-3 model, the seats were along the sides, facing each other.

Fokker Trimotor

Boeing Stratoliner

Martin Clipper

Short Empire Flying Boat

Handley Page HP 42 Airliner

it the 'tin goose' or the 'flying washboard'. But it carried only eight passengers and it was not comfortable.

Although various companies kept bringing out improved models of their aircraft, none of them was quite what the airlines needed. Then Donald Douglas went to work on the problem. He was an engineer who had started his own company in 1920, in the back room of a barber shop at Santa Monica, California. First he developed the DC-2. By 1936 he had developed the DC-3—and the airlines had their practical aeroplane.

Strangely enough, there was nothing particularly new about the DC-3. But never before had so many things been combined in one plane. It could carry twenty-one passengers at a speed of 185 m.p.h. It was safe, easy to fly, and comfortable. And it could be operated at much less cost than any other passenger airliner.

With the DC-3 setting the pace, the United States took the lead in transport aircraft production. DC-3's were used throughout the world. In time, other practical aircraft were built—the Short *Empire* flying boats, the Martin *Clippers*, the Boeing *Stratoliners*, the Lockheed *Constellations*. Airlines became big business, and flying became a common way of travel.

Sky-writing

Fire fighting

Ranching

Crop Dusting

AIRCRAFT AT WORK

All through the 1920's and 1930's, there were significant improvements in engines, instruments, and landing aids that made flying safer and far more comfortable. Among the most important were the retractable landing gear, the variable pitch propeller, and the Sperry Gyroscope automatic pilot. Engines with greater horsepower gave aircraft higher speeds. Designers learnt that streamlining lessened air resistance to a remarkable degree. New shapes and new devices made wings more efficient. As aluminium covered monoplanes replaced biplanes of wood and fabric, even the metal itself gradually improved. Propellers, too, were soon constructed of metal instead of wood.

Aircraft began to be put to work at many different kinds of tasks. The biggest job, of course, was carrying passengers, and airlines kept looking for ways to give them a more comfortable and speedier flight with as few stop-overs as possible. In 1930 Boeing Air Transport hired the first airline hostess to look after the comfort of passengers on San Francisco-Chicago flights. Other airlines soon followed Boeing's excellent example, and the hostess became a regular member of the crew on most airliners as they vied with each other to attract travellers.

Carrying mail and freight was another extremely important job. All sorts of goods were shipped by air, especially things that deteriorated quickly and had to be delivered without delay. In the cities, high above the tops of buildings, aircraft wrote advertising slogans in the sky with smoke. Photographers set up their cameras in aircraft, taking pictures from the air. Sometimes the pictures were used in making maps of various areas. On farms, aircraft proved themselves invaluable in spraying fields with insect-killing liquids and powders, and on ranches in the American West, planes were used to herd cattle together. In the forests, aircraft carrying tanks of water helped to fight fires. Aircraft dropped food and medicines to snow-bound villages, and helped to rescue people from floods.

Aircraft were doing so many jobs that a few military men began to think that they might be put to even wider use in time of war. An Italian general, Guilio Douthet, predicted that future wars would be won by countries with the strongest air forces. In the United States, General William L. 'Billy' Mitchell, assistant chief of the Army Air Service, had the same idea. He wanted the United States to set up an air force separate from the army and the navy. But most generals and admirals, in both Europe and America, believed in fighting wars the old way. Aircraft might be useful for scouting and observation, but wars were won by armies and navies, and aircraft should be under their control.

'Billy' Mitchell refused to give up. He said that bombers could sink the heaviest battleship afloat— even without scoring a direct hit. It was only necessary to drop bombs in the sea, close to an enemy ship. After the bomb exploded, the pressure of the water would smash a hole in the ship's side.

The admirals laughed. How could aircraft sink a giant battleship protected with heavy steel plates? But in 1921 General Mitchell persuaded them to let him test his ideas by bombing some captured German warships anchored in Chesapeake Bay. While military and government officials watched, the aircraft dropped their bombs—and the ships went down. Last to go down, on the last day of the test, was the great ship *Ostfriesland*. And the bombs that sank her had been dropped into the water.

Even after these tests, the government moved slowly to build up American military aviation, and Mitchell spoke out against army and navy leaders. In 1925 he was court-martialled and suspended from the army for five years. Twenty years later, after his death, he was restored to the service with the rank of major general and awarded the Congressional Medal of Honour for his 'service and foresight in aviation'.

Flood Rescue

At right is the sinking of the cruiser *Frankfurt*, one of the two captured German warships destroyed in General Mitchell's famous test of aerial bombing. The other ship was the huge dreadnought *Ostfriesland*, which some naval experts had called unsinkable. Below is an aerial photograph used in map-making.

Airline hostesses of 1930.

53

Britain's outnumbered Royal Air Force beat back the great German air attack and won the vital Battle of Britain.

AIR POWER

In Japan, in Italy, in Germany, military leaders carefully read the reports of General Mitchell's bombing experiments. They studied everything he wrote, and more and more often they used the words 'air power'. Japan was the first to test its aircraft, in fighting against the Chinese in Manchuria and the Russians in Manchukuo. Italy tested its aircraft when it attacked Ethiopia.

Meanwhile, Adolf Hitler had become ruler of Germany and was building up his air force, the *Luftwaffe*, for war. In 1936, he, too, got the chance to test his aircraft, when civil war broke out in Spain. Both Germany and Italy sent fighters and bombers to help General Franco's rebels, while Russia sent fighters to help the Spanish government.

Three years later Germany attacked Poland, starting World War II. The *Luftwaffe* roared over Europe, its dive-bombers screaming down on ground troops, its transports bringing up fuel and supplies, its fighters machine-gunning retreating armies and refugees. No one was safe. Bombs fell alike on soldiers and civilians – unarmed men, women, and children in cities and towns.

In August of 1940 Germany began the Battle of Britain, a battle fought entirely in the air. Day after day, for eighty-four days, German bombers blasted at England. More than 14,000 civilians were killed, more than 20,000 wounded. Germany had twice as many aircraft as Britain, and on one day almost a thousand of its bombers were in the air. But the Royal Air Force, flying *Spitfires* and *Hurricanes*, with skill and courage won the battle. After losing about 2,000 aircraft, Germany gave up. Never again did the *Luftwaffe* try to raid England by day in strength. Praising the young pilots who had saved their country, Britain's Prime Minister, Winston Churchill said in a memorable speech, 'Never in the field of human conflict has so much been owed by so many to so few.'

During World War II, parachutes dropped troops, arms, supplies and equipment, and were often coloured to identify types of equipment.

At sea, aircraft roared toward the enemy from giant aircraft carriers.

On December 7, 1941, Japanese naval aircraft, taking off from carriers, bombed the U.S. naval base at Pearl Harbour in Hawaii. In ninety minutes four battleships, a mine layer, and a target ship were sunk. Four other battleships, three cruisers, three destroyers, and a seaplane tender were damaged. Two thousand and eighty-six American naval men were killed, 749 were wounded. At the same time Japanese aircraft bombed Army Air Force bases at Hickham, Wheeler, and Bellows, destroying sixty-four planes and damaging eighty-six. America could no longer remain out of the war.

Pearl Harbour was one more lesson in the importance of air power in modern warfare. It was a lesson Britain and America learnt well. In time, their aircraft carried the war to Germany and Japan. Their bombers smashed at factories turning out the tools of war. Their fighters helped the ground forces. Their ambulance planes rushed the wounded to hospitals. Their transports carried men and materials to any corner of the world where they were needed. And it was an aeroplane that carried the atomic bomb, which gave aircraft even more power for death and destruction.

Japanese carrier-based bombers made a surprise attack on the American naval base at Pearl Harbor, Hawaii, in an attempt to crush the U.S. Navy's fighting strength with one mighty blow.

Mitsubishi Zero

Avro Lancaster

Republic P-47 Thunderbolt

Junkers JU.87 'Stuka'

AIRCRAFT OF WORLD WAR II

Although fifty-nine nations took part in World War II, the aerial war was fought almost entirely by American, British, Russian, German, and Japanese aircraft. At the beginning of the war, the German air force was the greatest in the world. Willy Messerschmitt, Germany's leading designer, produced the *Me. 109*, which was the *Luftwaffe*'s basic fighter. It had a top speed of about 354 m.p.h. and a good rate of climb, but was not too manoeuvrable. Later it was joined by the Focke-Wulf 190 and the twin-jet Messerschmitt Me. 262. Germany also had many bombers, such as the JU-87 *Stuka* dive bomber, and the Dornier and Heinkel bombers.

The most famous British fighter was the *Spitfire*. Its

outstanding manoeuvrability was one of the reasons the *Luftwaffe* was beaten in the Battle of Britain. Almost as famous was the Hawker *Hurricane*, which was superseded by the faster and more heavily armed Hawker *Typhoon* and *Tempest* fighters, which excelled in ground attack duties. The best heavy bomber of all was the British *Lancaster*, which was the one that carried the 22,000 lb. 'earthquake' bombs used against Germany. The outstanding aircraft of World War II was the de Havilland *Mosquito*. A twin-engined, wooden aircraft, this was used for fighting, bombing and reconnaissance.

The United States had a weak air force at the start of the war, and in 1940 President Roosevelt called for

Focke-Wulf FW.190

North American P-51 Mustang

Boeing B-17 Flying Fortress

Lockheed P-38 Lightning

the building of 50,000 aircraft a year. Production rose at an amazing rate, and in the one year of 1944, reached a total of 96,318 'planes. This was more than twice the number of aircraft that the United States had produced in the years from the Wright brothers' first flight to World War II.

Most famous of the American fighters was the P-51 *Mustang*, a long-range single-seater with a speed of 439 miles an hour. Just as famous were the heavy bombers—the B-17 *Flying Fortress*, the B-24 *Liberator*, and the B-29 *Superfortress*, which weighed 124,000 pounds and was a giant for its day. The B-17 carried out many of the mass bombing attacks that were a feature of World War II. Sometimes more than a thousand of them would go

roaring off to drop their bombs on an enemy target.

America's great air power helped to defeat the Japanese in the Pacific. The navy's carrier-based fighters, such as the F4F *Wildcat*, F6F *Hellcat*, and F4U *Corsair* battled enemy aircraft. B-24 *Liberators* and B-25 *Mitchells* attacked enemy ships, while B-29's bombed the mainland of Japan.

The Japanese air force proved surprisingly strong. Its outstanding aircraft were the navy fighter Mitsubishi Type 'O', known as the *Zero*, and Model 52, known as the *Zeke*. Japan had no heavy four-engine bombers, but used single- and twin-engine craft. Russia did little strategic bombing, but had fighters like the *Sturmovik* and the *Yak* to give direct support to ground troops.

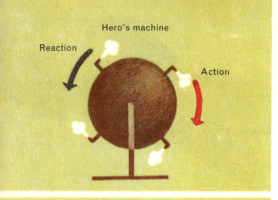

Hero's machine
Reaction
Action

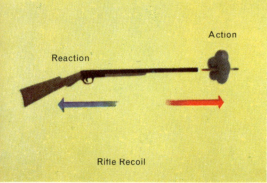

Action
Reaction
Rifle Recoil

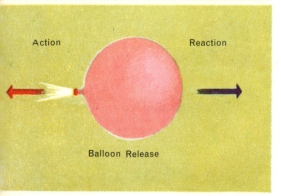

Action
Reaction
Balloon Release

Three illustrations of the scientific law that led to the development of jet planes.

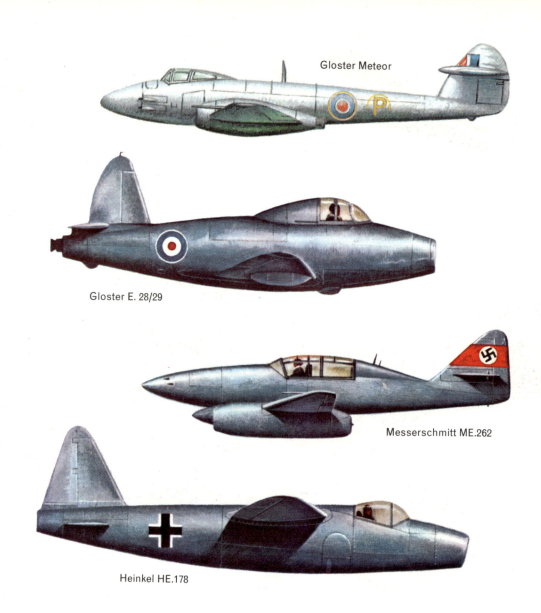

Gloster Meteor

Gloster E. 28/29

Messerschmitt ME.262

Heinkel HE.178

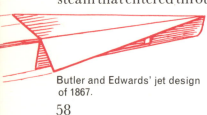

Butler and Edwards' jet design of 1867.

JETS—AIRCRAFT WITHOUT PROPELLERS

In 1944, less than a year before World War II ended, American and British pilots were startled by the attack of a German aircraft of new design. The speed of the aircraft–about 500 miles an hour–was amazing enough. But even more amazing was the fact that the aircraft had no propeller. Along with Britain's *Meteor*, this was the first jet propelled aircraft to go into combat, and represented a major step forward in the development of aircraft.

Not that there was anything new about the idea of jet propulsion. In ancient times, a Greek mathematician, Hero of Alexandria, constructed a jet propulsion machine. A hollow metal ball was mounted on two pipes so that it could spin freely, and filled with steam that entered through the pipes. Steam was allowed to escape from the ball through several jets, and the ball went spinning around. Hero's machine was proof of a scientific law: every action causes an equal reaction in the opposite direction. In Hero's machine, the escaping jets of steam furnished the action; the spinning of the ball was the reaction.

Hundreds of years later, scientists saw how the same law operated with everyday things. Firing a bullet from a rifle, for example, made the rifle 'kick back' in reaction to the action of the bullet. Another example was releasing a toy balloon filled with air. The balloon travelled as long as the air rushed out through its neck. The movement of the balloon was the reaction to the action of the air.

When men began to experiment with flying, some of them wondered how the law of action and reaction could be put to work to drive aircraft. As early as 1867 two Englishmen, Butler and Edwards, patented a design for an aircraft propelled by a jet of steam. In 1928 another Englishman, Frank Whittle, was writing about the use of gas turbine engines to drive aircraft by jet propulsion. At the same time, German, Italian,

58

French, and Swedish inventors were also thinking about the problem. And it was the Germans who built the world's first gas turbine jet plane, the Heinkel 178, which was flown at Rostock, Germany, in 1939.

The following year, the Italians attracted a great deal of attention with their Caproni-Campini N-1. Instead of a gas turbine engine, it used an ordinary piston engine to compress air. Although the N-1 was flown at a speed of 230 miles an hour, its design was not practical, and it was not put into production.

In 1941 the English flew their first jet, the Gloster E28/39, with a Whittle engine. From it developed the Gloster *Meteor* fighter, which was the only Allied jet to go into action in the war. Germany, on the other hand, in desperate need for fighters to counter the mass Allied bombing raids, produced several, in addition to the outstanding Me. 262. Although the jets came too late to change the course of the war, their high speed and rate of climb showed that they were the military aircraft of the future.

After the fighting was over the United States, Britain, and Russia pressed on hard with research in jets. When war broke out in Korea in 1950, the new military jets had their first real test in combat. The United States sent its F-86 *Sabre* jets to battle Russian MiG-15's used by Communist China. Both fighters soon proved their worth. The MiG had a very slightly higher speed and rate of climb, but the *Sabre* jet was a better all-round craft and was flown by more skilful pilots. Fourteen MiG's were shot down for every *Sabre* jet that was lost.

Aircraft without a propeller were definitely here to stay, not only for military use, but for every kind of commercial transport as well.

An F-86 Sabre jet closes in on a Russian MiG-15 during the fighting in Korea.

F-86 Sabre jet

MiG-15

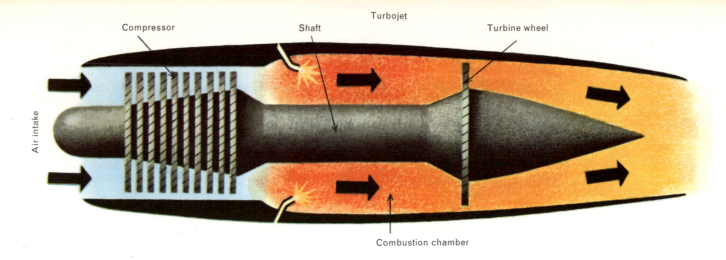

Turbojet

Compressor — Shaft — Turbine wheel

Air intake

Combustion chamber

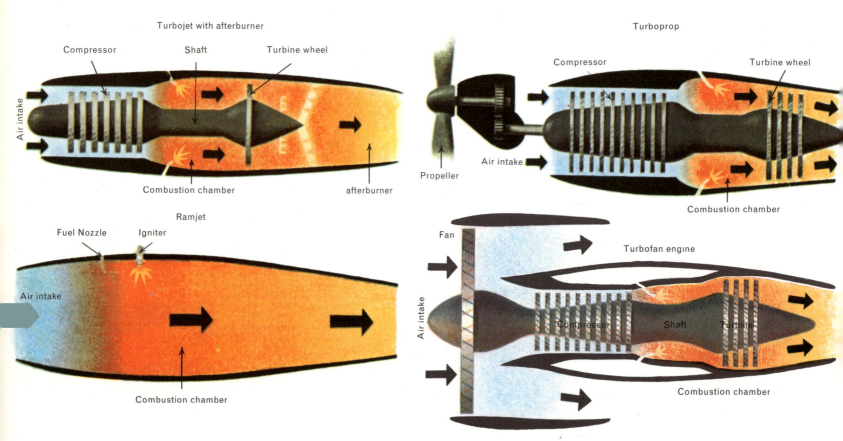

Turbojet with afterburner

Compressor — Shaft — Turbine wheel

Air intake

Combustion chamber — afterburner

Turboprop

Compressor — Turbine wheel

Propeller — Air intake

Combustion chamber

Ramjet

Fuel Nozzle — Igniter

Air intake

Combustion chamber

Fan

Turbofan engine

Air intake

Compressor — Shaft — Turbine

Combustion chamber

HOW JETS WORK

The most commonly used type of jet engine is the turbojet, and it works on a simple principle. Air is sucked in through the front of the engine, compressed, and mixed with fuel in the combustion chamber. The mixture is set on fire, and the burning, expanding gases rush out through the rear of the engine with great force. On the way, the gases strike fan blades on the turbine. The turbine turns the compressor, which is also a sort of fan with hundreds of blades that draw in the air and compress it.

Some turbojets have an after-burner. This is a pipe extending from the rear of the engine. In the pipe is another combustion chamber, where more fuel is added to the burning gases. The exhaust gases contain enough oxygen to burn the additional fuel with even greater

force. The after-burner needs so much fuel that it is used to give more power for take-off and for bursts of speed during combat manoeuvres.

Simplest of all jet engines is the ramjet, sometimes called the 'flying stove pipe'. It has almost no moving parts. But to operate, it must be moving at a high speed, and the aircraft must first be brought to this speed by another type of engine. The motion rams air into the open end of the engine, and no compressor is needed. Just as in the turbojet, fuel is added to the air, the mixture is set on fire, and the gases burst out through the tailpipe, or rear, of the engine. The ramjet can reach a higher speed than any other kind of jet engine, except the rocket.

The turboprop works the same way as the turbojet,

60

Above is the Bell P-59A Airacomet, the first American jet aircraft used during World War II for pilot training. The British de Havilland Comet I was the first jet airliner to be used in regular passenger service in 1952. At lower right is a Comet 4, fitted with more powerful engines for carrying more passengers over long distances.

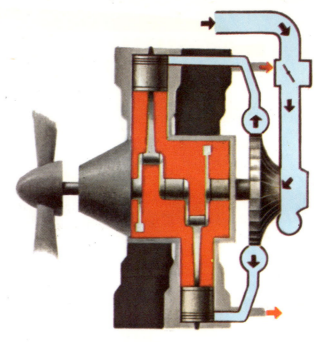

Cutaway view of piston engine, powered by petrol combustion, used on most propeller-driven aircraft. Arrows show the flow of fuel mixture. Pistons are arranged in a circle around the propeller shaft, or in a line, so that a number of them can be used to drive the same shaft.

but most of the force of the gases is used to turn a larger turbine. The turbine turns a propeller as well as a compressor. The turboprop aircraft stands halfway between the propeller-driven aircraft with an ordinary piston engine and the pure jet. It cannot go as fast or as high as a turbojet craft, but it can take off on a shorter runway and carry a load on less fuel. It is used on small passenger craft making short runs, and on cargo aircraft, where keeping down fuel costs is more important than high speeds.

The latest type of turbojet engine is the turbofan. These engines embody a large multi-blade fan at the front which throws back a powerful stream of air, some of which flows past the outside of the engine instead of through the combustion chambers. Turbofan engines are quieter and use much less fuel than ordinary turbojet engines.

The jet engine is better than the piston engine in many ways. It is faster, more powerful, lighter, smaller, and easier to install. It operates more efficiently at high altitudes and high speeds, and can use fuels such as paraffin, and diesel oil, as well as petrol. It produces less vibration and gives a much smoother ride. In 1952 Britain began the world's first jet airline service, flying the de Havilland *Comet* on regular runs between London and Johannesburg, South Africa.

Jets have brought some problems to the airlines. They need longer runways. They make an extremely loud noise at take-off. But, for long flights at high speeds, the jet engine works so well that it soon superseded the piston engine and turboprops.

Boeing B-52 Stratofortress.

JET FIGHTERS AND JET BOMBERS

The development in World War II of the atomic bomb, and the later development of the even more powerful 'hydrogen' bomb, gave mankind a weapon capable of destroying the world. Not unnaturally the air forces of Britain, the United States and Russia developed jet bombers to carry these new weapons.

In America, Boeing produced the six-jet, swept-wing B-47 *Stratojet*. With a range of 2,000 miles and a speed of 500 m.p.h., these represented a big step forward in bomber development.

The B-47's were superseded by the much bigger eight-jet B-52 *Stratofortress*. Weighing 490,000 lb. these huge machines usually carried two twenty-five megaton bombs, that is, two bombs–each with a destructive power equivalent to 25 million tons of conventional high explosives–equal to fifty times the destructive power of all the bombs dropped by the Royal Air Force throughout the whole of World War II. These bombers formed the backbone of America's 'deterrent' force for many years and helped to keep an uneasy peace through terror. Fortunately, B-52's never had to drop nuclear weapons in anger, but they have been used extensively in the Vietnam war in which they attacked enemy troop concentrations with conventional bombs.

Russia's counterpart to the B-52 was the Tu-20 *Bear*, a big swept-wing aircraft powered by four turboprop engines, which was enormously powerful.

Britain's heavy jet bombers included the Vickers *Valiant*, Avro *Vulcan* and Handley Page *Victor*. Because they did not need such a vast range, these bombers were much smaller than their American and Russian counterparts.

The *Vulcan* was the first bomber to use the delta wing configuration and has a service ceiling of 60,000 feet, a range of 4,000 miles and a maximum speed of 635 m.p.h. The *Victor* is one of the most aerodynamically advanced bombers in service. It has a crescent shaped wing, the sweep of which varies to give low drag at high speeds and yet retains good control at low speeds, through the reduced angle of sweep on the outer-wing panels.

A small number of supersonic bombers have been built and include the General Dynamics *Hustler* and the Russian Tu22 *Blinder*.

Vast numbers of jet fighters have been built to counter the bomber threat. Designed specifically for interception duties at high altitudes is the Lockheed F-104 *Starfighter*. This can climb to 50,000 feet in six minutes and has a maximum speed of over 1,450 m.p.h.

In service with the Royal Air Force is the BAC *Lightning*, a single-seater, twin-engined, all-weather interceptor. The two engines are mounted one above the other in the fuselage and give a top speed of about 1,400 m.p.h. at 40,000 feet.

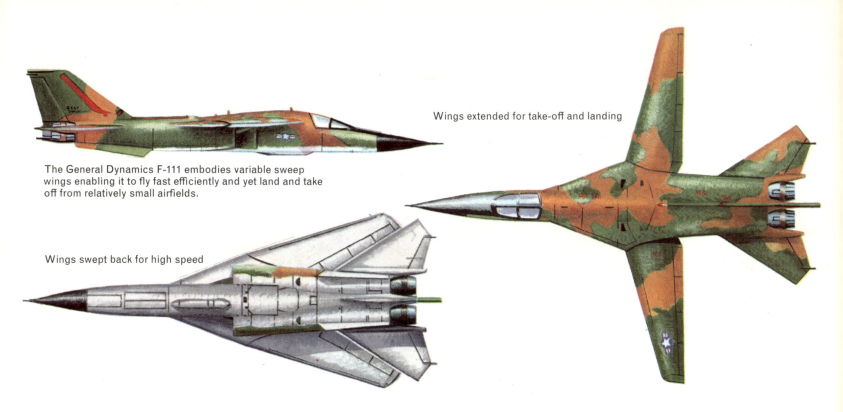

The General Dynamics F-111 embodies variable sweep wings enabling it to fly fast efficiently and yet land and take off from relatively small airfields.

Wings extended for take-off and landing

Wings swept back for high speed

Also in service with the Royal Air Force is the revolutionary Hawker-Siddeley *VTOL Harrier*. VTOL stands for Vertical Take Off and Landing. The *Harrier* can thus take off vertically, like a helicopter, which means that it can operate from virtually any small, flat, piece of ground. It achieves its helicopter-like ability by deflecting its jet exhaust downwards for vertical flight and rearward for normal flight.

In Russia a formidable series of fighters has followed the MiG-15 which did battle over Korea, including the MiG-17 and MiG-19, the first Soviet fighter capable of supersonic flight, and the MiG-21. The latest MiG is the 23, a twin-jet, single-seat multi-purpose aircraft, which has set officially-recognised speed records of over 1,850 m.p.h.

Nearly all jet fighters can carry bombs and rockets, in addition to their normal cannon or missile armament, for attacks on ground targets. For example, the McDonnell *Phantom*, a two-seat, carrier-borne aircraft, carries up to eight missiles for interception duties. For ground attack missions, however, under-wing loads of up to 16,000 lb. can be carried, including eighteen 750 lb. bombs, or twenty-four 500 lb. bombs, seven smoke bombs, eleven napalm bombs, or four Bullpup missiles and fifteen packs of smaller rockets.

It is not at all easy to design an aircraft that can both fly very fast and yet land and take-off extremely slowly. Swept wings are needed for high speeds and straight wings are essential for low speeds. In order to overcome this problem designers are turning to variable geometry aircraft, that is, aircraft on which the sweep of the wings can be radically altered in flight. The world's first combat aircraft to incorporate variable sweep-back wings was called the General Dynamics F-111, which has a top speed of 1,650 m.p.h. and yet can land on relatively small airfields.

Hawker Siddeley Harrier VTOL strike aircraft

Anglo-French Jaguar

Boeing 747 jumbo-jet

JUMBO-JETS AND SUPERSONIC AIRLINERS

The de Havilland *Comet* pioneered the introduction of jet flight for airline passengers, bringing a smoothness of flight not known before and a speed which cut flying times by over half. It was followed into service by the Boeing 707 and Douglas DC-8 families of jet airlines. These aircraft are much bigger and, with swept wings and more powerful engines, are even faster than the early *Comets*. Russia produced the Tu 104 *Camel* airliner which has been followed by other, improved jets.

The latest Boeing 707 is the model 707-320C. Powered by four turbofan engines each developing an 18,000 lb. thrust, this can carry up to 202 passengers nearly 4,000 miles. The latest DC-8 development is the *Super Sixty* series, the biggest of which has a stretched fuselage accommodating up to 259 passengers, while the long range version has a range of 6,000 miles with the maximum payload.

Perhaps the best of the first generation of jet airliners is Britain's VC-10. This jet has its four powerful engines mounted at the rear of the fuselage, giving a quiet ride to passengers in the luxuriously furnished cabin. The VC-10 was especially designed for the England-to-South Africa air routes, which have relatively small airfields, and thus has exceptionally good take-off and landing characteristics. Russia has also produced an airliner with four jets at the back, known as the Il-62.

Jet airlines are, of course, extremely expensive to operate and to help make them pay their way, the passengers have to be crowded close together in long and relatively narrow cabins.

A new range of wide-bodied airliners has brought spaciousness to jet flight, as well as speed. The first of these new jumbo-jets can carry up to 490 passengers, but most have seats for only 345 passengers, arranged in a series of attractively furnished cabins. On the 747 a small 'upstairs' cabin behind the flight deck can be used for business conferences or as a rest lounge.

Equally spacious and comfortable are the Mc-Donnell-Douglas DC-10 and the Lockheed 1011 *TriStar* tri-jet 'airbuses'.

The big advantage of air travel is speed, and with military aircraft flying faster than sound daily, it was inevitable that sooner or later supersonic airliners would be developed. Supersonic airliners are difficult to design, require immensely powerful engines and are extremely expensive to build.

Upper deck cabin on the Boeing 747

Because of the great expense, Britain and France co-operated with one another to produce the West's first supersonic airliner. The result is the Anglo-French *Concorde*. Designed to fly at twice the speed of sound, that is around 1,400 m.p.h., at a height of 60,000 feet, the *Concorde* can carry up to 144 passengers over ranges of up to 4,000 miles. It has a delta-wing and in flight looks rather like one of the paper darts made at school. To give the pilot an adequate view during take-off and landing, the needle-pointed nose can be hinged downwards.

The *Concorde* is powered by four Olympus turbojet engines each of which develops a 35,080 lb. thrust, which can be increased to 38,300 lb. by the use of reheat. The *Concorde* is 193 feet long and has a wingspan of 84 feet. Its maximum take-off weight is 367,000 lb. To help maintain the correct balance as the aircraft accelerates to supersonic flight, fuel is pumped from tanks in the front of the wing to tanks at the rear.

Similar in general shape and size to the *Concorde* is Russia's Tu-144, which was the first supersonic airliner to take to the air and the first to fly faster than sound. The Tu-144 is designed to cruise at 1,550 m.p.h., which is slightly faster than the *Concorde*. Like that of the *Concorde*, the nose can be lowered to provide a better view during landing.

Boeing supersonic airliner

In America, a design competition for the most promising supersonic airliner was won by the Boeing Company, who presented a design featuring a variable-sweep wing. Further investigation indicated that this was too heavy and complicated, and Boeing are currently refining a project with a fixed-sweep delta-wing and a conventional tail. This they now consider to be the most efficient and economical design.

The U.S. supersonic airliner is to fly at 1,800 m.p.h. and, to withstand the extreme temperatures generated at this speed, will be constructed of titanium.

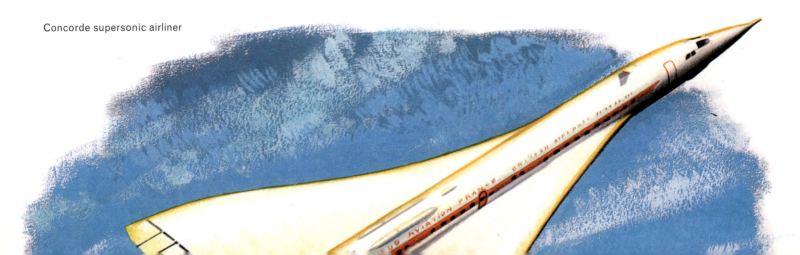
Concorde supersonic airliner

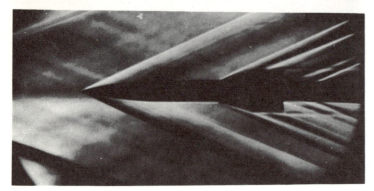

The photographs above show the shape of shock waves produced by an experimental model in a wind tunnel.

THE SOUND BARRIER

When Ernst Mach began his experiments, around 1870, the aeroplane had not yet been invented. There were few man-made things in the world that moved really fast. Still, the young Austrian professor of physics could not help wondering about the relationship of speed, sound, air and gases. Like other scientists, he knew that sound travels at different speeds, depending on temperature and air pressure. At sea level, for instance, with the temperature at 59 degrees Fahrenheit, the speed of sound is 761 miles an hour.

But what happens when an object moves swiftly through the air, approaching the speed of sound? Mach wanted to find out. He borrowed a cannon and took photographs of shells passing through the air. He learned that the shells pushed the air, which piled up in shock waves. And years later, to honour Mach, engineers used 'Mach numbers' to indicate the speed of aircraft. Mach 1 means that an aeroplane is flying at the speed of sound, Mach 2 at twice the speed of sound, and so on.

Trouble with Mach 1 began in World War II. Some pilots approached the speed of sound while making power dives. Suddenly the controls no longer worked and the aircraft shook with a terrible vibration. Few pilots lived to tell of the strange behaviour of their aircraft. Usually the machine was shattered to pieces in the air, or it dived, screaming, to the ground.

At first no one knew exactly what had gone wrong. But as engineers and designers worked with aircraft approaching the speed of sound, they began to understand. An aircraft causes pressure waves which travel through the air with the speed of sound. In fact, the

Aircraft travelling below the speed of sound (left) causes waves in the air (as shown bottom left). But the waves, which move at the speed of sound, stay well ahead of the machine. As the aircraft reaches the speed of sound (centre) it catches up with the waves, which pile up and form a wall. At supersonic speeds (right) the aircraft leaves the turbulent shock waves behind.

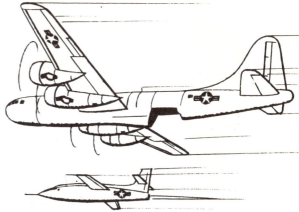

The rocket-powered Bell X-1, first aeroplane to fly faster than the speed of sound. It could travel only a few minutes on its own power, so it was carried aloft by a B-29 'mother plane'. At 30,000 feet it was released and the rockets were fired. After flying through the sound barrier it coasted to earth.

pressure waves *are* sound. A slow-flying aircraft pushes pressure waves far ahead of it, at least as far ahead as the aircraft can be heard. The waves part the air for the passage of the aircraft. But when the aircraft itself reaches the speed of sound, it catches up with the waves. Air piles up like a wall, forming a sound barrier.

If aircraft were to fly safely at the speed of sound, they would have to break through the sound barrier. American designers attacked the problem, and produced the Bell X-1, an experimental rocket aircraft. It did not take off from the ground, but was launched from another aeroplane. A number of trial flights were made at the U.S. Air Force base at Muroc Dry Lake, in the California desert.

On the morning of October 14, 1947, Captain Charles Yeager climbed into the cockpit of the X-1. The aircraft, attached to a big bomber, was taken high into the air and released. Gingerly, Yeager fired the first barrel of his rocket motor. The X-1 began to accelerate. Then Yeager fired the remaining three motors. The needle on the Mach-meter started to move round the dial . . . . 92 . . . . 94. The X-1 began to buffet and no longer felt stable, but there was little Yeager could do now. The needle continued to revolve . . . . 96 . . . . 98. Then, suddenly, the Mach-meter went crazy and swung right off the dial and back, and the buffeting stopped. Calmly, Yeager reported this to his escorting

chase 'planes, and then switched off the rockets. The X-1 then began a long spiral glide back to base. As he landed, Yeager glanced at his watch. It was just fourteen minutes since he had been released from the *Superfortress* bomber. In these fourteen minutes, however, history had been made and the sound barrier broken for the first time.

Britain broke the sound barrier in 1948, with the de Havilland DH-108, a picture of which is shown on the opposite page.

Since these pioneering days, breaking the sound barrier has become an everyday occurrence, until today we are preparing for the introduction of supersonic passenger carrying airlines.

First aeroplane to exceed 1,000 m.p.h. was Britain's Fairey Delta 2.

Convair B-58 Hustler

Pressurised suits are needed in modern aircraft which fly at high altitudes, where there is little oxygen in the atmosphere.

NEW FRONTIERS, NEW PIONEERS

Moving more swiftly than sound, aircraft were flashing through the thin upper atmosphere, far beyond the birds flying in the lower air. Men had outdistanced the birds they had once envied. They could fly faster, farther, higher. And, to meet the challenge of new frontiers of flight, they changed the shapes of aeroplanes, creating strange new forms of aircraft.

Among the new forms were the swept-back wing and the delta wing. Another was the 'coke bottle' or 'wasp waist' design of Richard Whitcomb, an American scientist. Whitcomb knew that great power was needed to push aircraft through the sound barrier, because of the tremendous drag—the force that tends to hold aircraft back. The drag was caused by shock waves, and Whitcomb believed that most of it came from a shock wave at the rear of the wing. Air streaming swiftly over the top of the wing crashed into the slower-moving air at the rear, sometimes twisting the aircraft like a giant hand. Some way had to be found to make this crash less violent.

Using mathematics, Whitcomb worked out the most nearly perfect shape for a supersonic aircraft. He pinched in the fuselage, or 'waist', at the point where the wings are joined to it. He added bulges to the rear of the fuselage. And when aircraft of 'coke bottle' design were tested, they slipped through the sound barrier more easily. They had less vibration than other aircraft, and needed less power.

As new kinds of aircraft entered the new frontiers of flight, there was a new kind of pioneer—the scientist-test pilot—to fly them. Like the pioneers of the early days of aviation, these men explored strange and unknown territory, often at the risk of their lives. But there were some important differences. The pioneers of the past flew at low speeds and low altitudes. They often crashed and many were injured or killed. Some, though, walked away unhurt. Test pilots, flying at supersonic speeds high above the earth, could not afford to make mistakes. Few of them ever got a second chance.

And so, behind every test flight, there were long hours of preparation, for both man and machine. Scientists, designers, and engineers performed experiments and made calculations. Inspite of all the care and planning, there was still danger. No one could say for certain how any new aircraft would behave in actual flight—until after the test pilot had taken it up.

Even then, strange things could happen. Charles Yeager, the first man to break the sound barrier, was flying the Bell X-1A six years later. After travelling at Mach 2, or 1,650 miles an hour, he dropped back to a lower speed. Suddenly the plane went out of control. It tumbled across the sky, and Yeager's head slammed against the canopy of the cockpit. He became unconscious. Before he recovered, the plane had fallen 51,000 feet—almost ten miles—in fifty-one seconds. Luckily, it righted itself and went into a glide. Yeager landed safely, but he never knew exactly what had gone wrong. He could only guess that he had cut off his power too fast and had gone into a stall at high speed.

Other pilots have had similar experiences. And, as long as there are new aircraft to test, there will be danger, for there has always been and always will be danger in exploring the unknown.

68

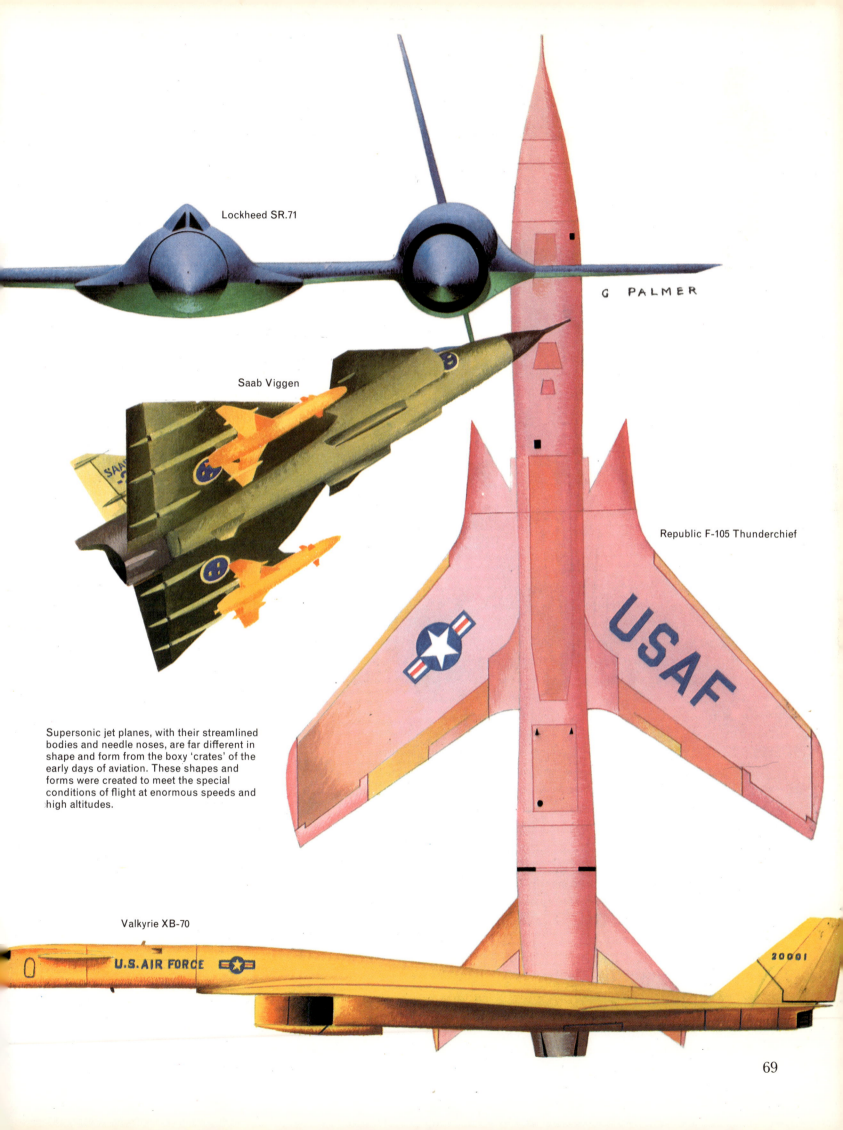

Lockheed SR.71

Saab Viggen

Republic F-105 Thunderchief

G PALMER

USAF

Supersonic jet planes, with their streamlined bodies and needle noses, are far different in shape and form from the boxy 'crates' of the early days of aviation. These shapes and forms were created to meet the special conditions of flight at enormous speeds and high altitudes.

Valkyrie XB-70

U.S. AIR FORCE

20001

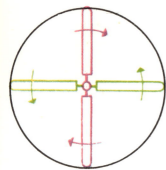

View from above of two helicopter rotors shows how they revolve in opposite directions to give stability and control.

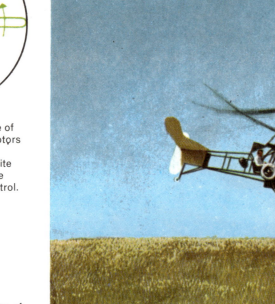

Louis Breguet, one of the first men to fly a helicopter, built this improved model years later.

THE HELICOPTERS

High speed was the aim of most aeroplane designers during the 1930's and 1940's, and finally they produced aircraft without propellers that raced the sound of their own flight. However, a few other designers were working on the helicopter, an aircraft without wings, for a different kind of flight. These designers were not interested in high speed. In fact, they wanted to develop a craft that could move at very low speeds and even hang motionless in the air. They also wanted it to move straight up and down, and fly forward, backward, and sideways.

The task seemed a fairly simple one, for the principles of the helicopter had been known for many years. By mounting a large, rotating propeller with wide blades— called a rotor—on top of the craft, it could be driven up and down. And yet the problems were not as simple as they seemed, and successful helicopters were not built until after aeroplanes were a common sight in the sky.

The first design for a helicopter was made about 1500 by Leonardo da Vinci. He may even have constructed a small model, powered by a spring mechanism. He wrote in one of his notebooks that if the curving blade were turned at great speed, it would be able 'to form a screw in the air, and climb high'. After Leonardo's death, his plans for a helicopter, like the rest of his scientific writings and sketches, were lost to the world for 278 years. Curiously, it was only

thirteen years before Leonardo's notebooks were discovered that men again began to experiment with helicopters.

By 1784 a simple helicopter toy had reached Europe from China, where it had been known for a long time. Two Frenchmen named Launoy and Bienvenu built and flew a 'Chinese top' of their own, using feathers for propellers. This interested George Cayley, the English inventor, who made a similar one for himself. Cayley later built a different type with a metal propeller that flew as high as ninety feet, and designed a remarkable converti-plane—a combination helicopter and aeroplane.

Excitement about helicopters spread over Europe, and in 1828 Vittorio Sarti, an Italian, drew up a cleverly designed craft. In 1863, the Vicomte de Ponton d'Amécourt of France built a model helicopter powered by steam. It failed to fly, but the Vicomte had better success with some models driven by clockwork. With a sailor, Gabrielle de La Landelle, and a balloonist who went by the name of Nadar, he formed a society to interest people in helicopters. They produced no practical aircraft, but turned out a number of unusual designs. One of them, by de La Landelle, looked much like a ship.

In 1878 Enrico Forlanini, an Italian engineer, was able to get a steam-driven model to rise as high as forty-two feet. Very little more was done with helicopters until 1907. In that year the Breguet brothers, Louis and Jacques, built a helicopter that lifted Louis into the air. Another French inventor, Paul Cornu, successfully flew another helicopter a few weeks later. Although the Breguet machine was the first to take off with a man, it was not a 'free' flight, as four men held the ground support poles—one under each of the four great rotors. Although this did not help to lift the machine, it certainly aided its stability in the air. The Cornu helicopter, on the other hand, flew without any help from, or connection with, the ground. Thus, to Paul Cornu goes the honour of making the first helicopter flight.

It must be emphasised that both the Breguet and Cornu helicopters were crude, experimental machines and although they flew, they were by no means practical. Helicopters posed many problems.

Leonardo da Vinci sketched this helicopter design around 1500.

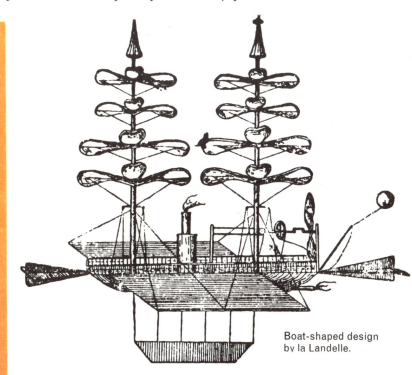

Boat-shaped design by la Landelle.

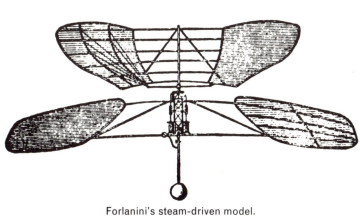

Forlanini's steam-driven model.

Sarti's design of 1828 was advanced for its day.

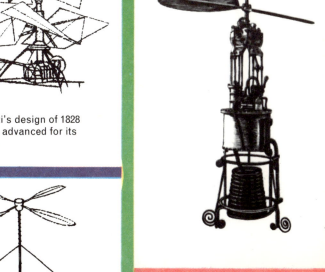

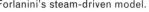

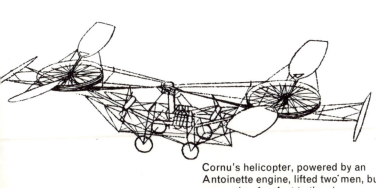

Cornu's helicopter, powered by an Antoinette engine, lifted two men, but rose only a few feet in the air.

Model helicopter by Cayley, based on the one made by Launoy and Bienvenu in 1784.

Ponton d'Amécourt's 1863 model for a steam-driven helicopter. The little machine was beautifully designed, with some of its engine parts made of aluminium. Even so, it was too heavy to fly.

Sikorsky Sky-crane

Cierva's Autogiro

Focke-Achgelis FW-61

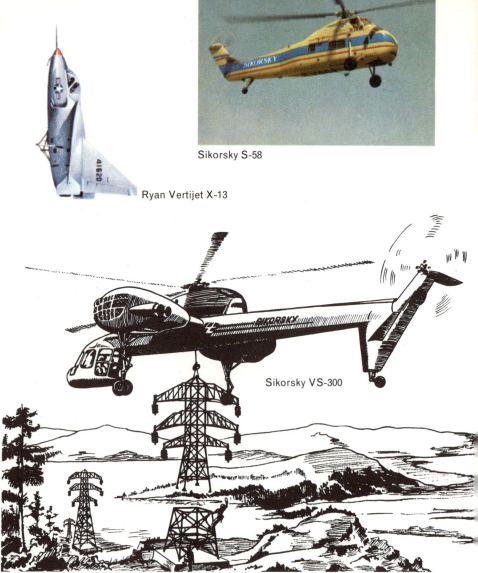

Ryan Vertijet X-13

Sikorsky S-58

Sikorsky VS-300

WHIRLYBIRDS, TILT-WINGED AIRCRAFT, JET LIFT AIRCRAFT

Inspite of all the problems, the men who wanted to make helicopters refused to give up. Juan de la Cierva, a Spaniard, put together a craft he called an Autogiro. It was not a helicopter, because the big rotor which lifted it into the air was not turned directly by a motor. Cierva's Autogiro had an ordinary engine driving a propeller. This pulled the machine along, when the flow of air caused the rotor to revolve and create lift.

The Autogiro could take off and land in a small space, but it could not move straight up and down, or hover motionless. While it could fly more slowly than the ordinary aeroplane, it was hard to control at low speeds. Cierva built his first Autogiro in 1923, and a number of them were produced in the years that followed.

With the coming of the helicopter, the Autogiro disappeared from the skies – and by 1938 the helicopter was well on its way. In Germany the Focke-Achgelis FW-61 flew higher than 11,000 feet and stayed aloft

for eighty minutes. Besides flying slowly, it could reach a speed of about seventy-six miles an hour. The FW-61 had two rotors mounted on outriggers, one at each side, and an ordinary propeller in front for forward thrust.

At the same time, Igor Sikorsky was busy with helicopters. He was in America, where he had settled after leaving Russia. Sikorsky had dreamed of helicopters since he was a boy, when he had seen a picture of Leonardo's design. After some early experiments, he put aside his dream to work on aeroplanes. Now he was again experimenting. In 1939 he solved the problem of torque, balancing the pull – or torque – of the rotor with a small propeller mounted on the left side of the body, near the tail. Sikorsky's craft did everything a helicopter was supposed to do, and did it well.

Soon other inventors solved the torque problem in different ways. Some used two rotors, mounted one above the other, revolving in opposite directions. Others

Boeing-VERTOL Chinook twin-turbine army transport helicopter

LTV XC-142 Tilt Wing Transport

Dornier DO.31 VTOL Jet Lift Transport

Rotor blade arrangements

used two rotors mounted at the ends of the craft.

With their slow speed and ability to land almost anywhere, helicopters can go many places where ordinary aircraft cannot. They proved their value in World War II to a limited extent, but the helicopter really came of age during the war in Korea. In this conflict they were used for rescue and air ambulance duties on an unprecendented scale. In three years they carried over 23,000 casualties, and it is estimated that over half of these would have died if helicopters had not been available to take them to hospital quickly.

Helicopters have also been used extensively in Vietnam, where they have literally been employed as the cavalry of the air.

Helicopters, however, are complicated and expensive. Also, they are not very fast. Designers, therefore, have been investigating other ways of enabling aircraft to take-off and land vertically, and yet fly faster in normal flight.

One way of doing this is to rotate the engines. For take-off, the engines point upward, and the propellers lift the aircraft straight up. Once airborne, however, the engines are tilted forward, and the machine then flies like a conventional aeroplane. On other 'convertiplanes' the entire wing is hinged and tilts in flight.

Yet another way is to use jet engines to provide the lift for vertical flight. The biggest aircraft using jet lift is the German Dornier Do. 31. This has pods on the wings, each containing four small jet engines, pointing downwards. These are used for vertical take-offs and landings. For level flight, the lift engines are switched off, and the main propulsion engines under the wing are used quite conventionally.

Hawker Harrier VTOL strike aircraft directs its jet exhaust downward through rotating nozzles for vertical flight, rearward for normal flight.

VC.10

INSTRUMENTS OF FLIGHT

When the Wright brothers made their first flight, they had only three instruments. These were a stop watch, for timing the flights; an anemometer, for measuring the force of the wind; and a counter, which showed the number of times per minute the engine turned the propellers. A year later, when they were testing another aircraft, they added a new instrument. It was a piece of string.

The string was tied to the crossbar underneath the front elevator, and it streamed straight backward as long as the aircraft moved forward. But if the aircraft slipped sideways, the string, too, would be blown to one side. By watching the string, the Wrights could guard against slipping into a dangerous tailspin while making turns. It was a simple but effective device.

The pilots in the early days of aviation flew 'by the seat of their pants'—by the feel of the controls, by their sense of balance, by what they could see and hear with their eyes and ears. As aircraft improved and flights became longer, they needed more and more instruments. There were instruments to check the performance of engines, and to aid navigation. Instruments made possible night flying and blind flying in bad weather.

With the development of the supersonic jet, the pilot's job became even harder. The jet engine itself was simpler than the piston engine, and required fewer controls and instruments. But at high speeds things happened so fast that pilots could not keep up with them.

This was especially true for men flying jet fighters.

Flight deck of the Boeing 707 jet passenger airliner, with its great number and variety of instrument gauges. The captain sits at the left and the co-pilot at his right.

The Vertical Speed Indicator gives the speed at which an aircraft is climbing or dropping. In level flight, the indicator registers zero.

The Altitude Horizon Indicator is an electrically-driven gyroscopic device that tells the pilot whether his aircraft is flying level, upside down, or tilted in any direction.

Not only was it extremely difficult to aim and fire at an enemy aircraft, but if a pilot missed, the high speeds involved meant that it was rarely possible to have a second chance. To help the pilot, equipment was made that guided the fighter towards the enemy. Later, equipment was developed that not only automatically guides a fighter to an enemy aircraft, but fires its rockets when it is within range.

The next step seemed to be to eliminate the pilot, and this, in effect, came about when guided anti-aircraft rockets were developed. Fired from the ground, these travel at speeds of up to 2,000 m.p.h. and can seek out and destroy enemy aircraft flying as high as 100,000 feet.

The latest instruments of flight are a series of 'black boxes' that control and guide aircraft so accurately that automatic landings can be made in weather too bad for pilots to land in on their own.

As aircraft become more and more complicated, new instruments are being developed to help the pilot in his job. The Automatic Dead Reckoning Set computes the aircraft's position at any time during a flight. Information is fed into this Data Setting Box, and a separate dial indicates course and distance to the target or base.

The Airspeed Indicator tells the pilot how fast his aircraft is moving through the air.

The Altimeter shows the altitude at which the aircraft is flying. The three pointers indicate hundreds, thousands, and tens of thousands of feet. On later altimeters the height is shown in figures, as on a car milometer.

The Direction Indicator is a magnetic compass. One arm is set to the course desired by the pilot. When the other arm is lined up with it, the aircraft is on that course.

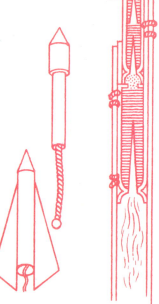

Designs for war rockets driven by gunpowder, as shown in a book on fireworks published in 1747.

Rockets were used in the bombardment of Fort McHenry.

THE ROCKET'S RED GLARE

During the War of 1814, a young American named Francis Scott Key watched anxiously through the night as ships of the British navy bombarded Fort McHenry in Baltimore. In the flash of bursting bombs and rockets he occasionally caught a glimpse of the American flag still flying over the fort.

The next day he wrote down what he had seen in a song called *The Star-Spangled Banner*, which actually became the national anthem of the United States. Millions of Americans have since sung of 'the rockets' red glare' which 'gave proof through the night that our flag was still there'.

During the 1600's, war rockets were launched from a portable launching ramp which could be set up anywhere on a battlefield.

The rockets that burst over Fort McHenry were artillery rockets with explosive heads, invented in 1805 by Sir William Congreve, a British army officer. Even then the rockets had already had a long history. The first use of rockets for war was about the year 1100, when the Chinese used gunpowder to propel missiles.

The first attempt to fly a rocket aircraft also took place in China. Around 1500, Wan-Hoo attached a saddle to two large kites and tied forty-seven rockets to them. He got into the saddle and signalled to forty-seven men, who lit all the rockets at the same time. There was a great explosion and Wan-Hoo was killed.

Over the years, European armies used rockets from time to time. Congreve's rockets were used in the Napoleonic Wars as well as in the War of 1812. In 1826 William Hale, an American, invented a rocket with vanes on the tail, an improvement over the usual stick rocket. The vanes gave it a steadier flight, and the U.S. Army used this type of rocket in the Mexican War.

The development of breech-loaded, rifled cannon, giving increased rate of fire and improved accuracy, however, ended the use of rockets for war at this stage. Thus, in World War I, rockets were used mainly for signalling, or as flares to light up battle areas during night fighting.

At sea, rockets were also used for flares and signalling, and to carry lines between ships, and between ship and shore during rough weather.

But Dr. Robert Goddard, a young American physics

The first man-carrying jet aeroplane was powered by rockets. It made a short flight in Germany in 1928. The rocket-propelled glider shown here flew in 1929.

by the force of the explosion pushing against the air. Dr. Goddard ended his report by predicting that rockets could be made powerful enough to reach the moon. Newspapers carried stories of Dr. Goddard's plans for a space rocket, and people laughed at the crazy idea.

Dr. Goddard paid no attention to the laughter. He went on with his work, and in 1926 he was ready to test the world's first liquid-fuel rocket. It flew 184 feet at a speed of sixty miles an hour. Three years later he was able to send up a rocket that carried a barometer and a camera. In 1928, an Opel rocket aircraft, the first jet-propelled aeroplane to carry a man, made a short flight in Germany.

On May 31, 1935, Dr. Goddard sent a rocket, controlled by a gyroscope, blasting 7,500 feet into the air at a speed of 700 miles an hour. He was well on the way to solving the problems of rocket flight when he died in 1945. But he had done his work quietly, and his name meant little to those who read of his death.

Dr. Robert H. Goddard, American rocket pioneer, just before he launched the first liquid-fuel rocket in 1926.

Cutaway view of a liquid-fuel rocket showing fuel tanks, pumps and valves, and combustion chamber. Fuels such as alcohol and paraffin are generally used, in combination with liquid oxygen.

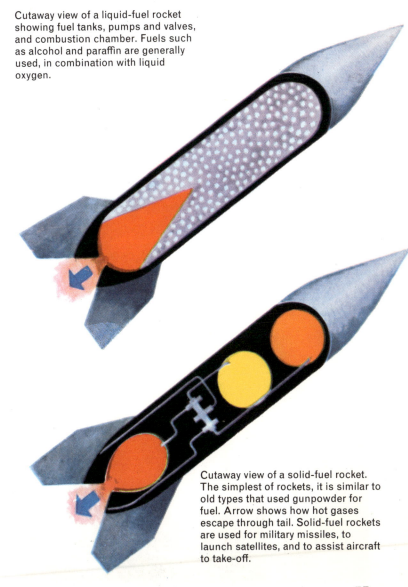

Cutaway view of a solid-fuel rocket. The simplest of rockets, it is similar to old types that used gunpowder for fuel. Arrow shows how hot gases escape through tail. Solid-fuel rockets are used for military missiles, to launch satellites, and to assist aircraft to take-off.

WEAPONS OF VENGEANCE

In World War II, rockets were again sent into battle. Fitted with explosive warheads, they were used by both sides in many ways. They were launched from aircraft, from trucks, and from tanks. They were also launched from ships, laying down depth charges to destroy submarines. They were launched from amphibious craft, against beaches held by the enemy. They were launched from bazookas, which were fired from the shoulders of infantrymen.

But the Germans, who had carefully followed the work of Robert Goddard, had some new ideas, and they took the lead in rockets as well as in jet propulsion. In 1944 they were ready to launch their *Vergeltungswaffen*–weapons of revenge.

The first of these weapons, the V-1, was not a rocket, but a small jet aeroplane. It was controlled mechanically, and needed no pilot. The V-1's were set off in Europe, flew up to 150 miles over the English Channel and nose-dived to earth in London, loaded with about 2,000 pounds of explosives. They were nicknamed 'buzz bombs' because of the noise they made.

The V-1 had a speed of about 400 miles an hour, and many hundreds were shot down by fighters and anti-aircraft guns. The Germans then used the V-2, a ballistic rocket with a one-ton warhead. It had a range of 200 miles and travelled at a speed of 3,000 miles an hour. The V-2 brought death silently, dropping from a height of fifty miles. About 1,000 of them landed in England, killing some 3,000 people.

The Germans also produced a rocket-propelled aeroplane, the Messerschmitt Me. 163. It was generally towed into action, and landed on a skid after not more than ten minutes in the air. The stubby little aeroplane, with two cannons, was used with great effectiveness as an interceptor-fighter against bombers. Germany's

V-1 buzz bombs killed more than 6,000 people in England.

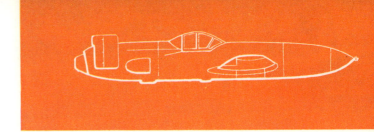

The Japanese Baka rocket bomb.

ally, Japan, had the *Baka*, which was basically a large rocket bomb. It was guided by a *kamikaze*, or 'suicide pilot', who was killed when the bomb exploded. The men who flew these were extraordinarily brave.

After the war, the United States and Russia, aided by several distinguished German scientists, made missiles of their own. Some travelled by rocket power, while others used jet engines. Still others employed a combination of rockets and jet engines, with the rockets furnishing the power for quick take-offs which turned out to be very effective.

Both the United States and Russia produced various kinds of missiles designed for different purposes. Among them were long-range missiles that could guide themselves by the position of the stars and find their targets in far distant places. Anti-aircraft missiles, on the other hand, could seek out the enemy by following the heat waves given off by an aircraft's engines.

Missiles were rapidly made with a longer and longer range. The ICBMs, or Intercontinental Ballistics Missiles, can travel over 5,000 miles. Leaping from continent to continent, passing over oceans, they can deliver death and destruction to any point on earth. Inevitably, these have caused a revolution in warfare.

But if rockets can be used in times of war, they can also be used in times of peace. For rockets carry their own oxygen and do not need to get it from the air. They can thus operate well beyond the earth's atmosphere, in the vacuum of space. With the aid of rockets, man was

The Messerschmitt Me. 163, a German rocket fighter, could fly at a speed of nearly 600 miles an hour.

able to begin probing space. At first the rockets did little more than go straight up, before falling back to earth. But, as more powerful rockets were made, higher and higher speeds were reached until, in October 1957, Russia was able to put the world's first artificial satellite, called Sputnik 1, into orbit. This historic event can be regarded as man's first step to the moon – a step helped by the weapons of revenge made in World War II.

After World War II the United States and Russia took the lead in rocketry. Both countries have developed an extensive range of missiles, some examples of which are pictured here. They are not drawn to the same scale.

Minuteman (U.S.A.)   Scrag (U.S.S.R.)   Poseidon (U.S.A.)   Griffon (U.S.S.R.)   Sparton (U.S.A.)

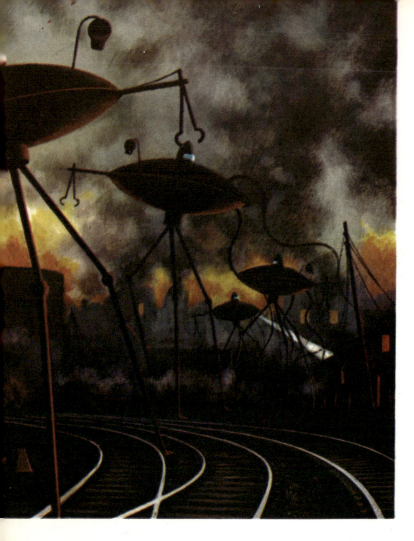

Years before the first space satellite, men wondered about space travel and about life on other planets. The illustration above of H. G. Wells' story 'The War of the Worlds' shows a Martian attack on the earth. The Martians, described as 'squid-like' creatures, moved about in machines embodying long mechanical legs. In 1938 a radio broadcast of a play based on this story frightened many Americans, who believed that Martians had actually landed on the earth.

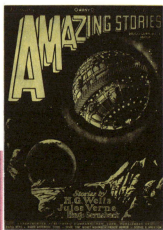

'Amazing Stories', first published in 1927, often featured stories of space travel. Even before this, comics like the one at left carried tales of adventure in the sky.

A scene from 'Journey to the Moon', a film about space travel made in 1902 by Georges Méliès, a French film pioneer. The huge cannon is about to fire a man-carrying spacecraft at the moon.

THE ADVENTURE OF SPACE

And so men were rulers of the air, which had once belonged to the birds, and to devils and gods. But still they were not satisfied. They looked upward, beyond the clouds, beyond the ocean of air around the earth, to the enormous regions of outer space. They looked at the moon and the planets and the even more distant stars. With the telescope, the camera, the radio, and other instruments, they searched for the secrets of the heavens–and they wondered. Could they learn to travel through space, as they had learnt to travel through the air?

True, men had wondered about space travel before. In the second century, the Greek writer Lucian wrote of an imaginary trip to the moon. So did Cyrano de Bergerac, a Frenchman, in 1640. That same year John Maynard, an Englishman, wrote *A Discourse Concerning a New World & Another Planet in Two Bookes*. In 1865 Jules Verne, the father of science-fiction, wrote *From the Earth to the Moon* and *Around the Moon*, in which a satellite circled the moon, carrying three men and two dogs. In 1898 H. G. Wells wrote *The War of the Worlds*, which told of creatures from Mars attacking the earth in space ships. And novels and science-fiction magazines carried many tales about space travel to the far places of the universe.

The first really scientific book connected with space travel was Professor Goddard's *A Method of Reaching Extreme Altitudes*. In 1923 Hermann Oberth, a German mathematician, wrote *The Rocket in Interplanetary Space*. When the remarkable little book was printed again in 1929, he called it *The Way to Space Travel*.

Up to this time, stories of space ships were little more than fantastic dreams. But Goddard's experiments showed that rockets could operate without air. They

This sketch, drawn by Méliès in preparation for the film, shows the landing of the spacecraft on the moon. Méliès paid no attention to the fact that there is no air on the moon for men to breathe.

After World War II, scientists reached greater and greater heights in their experiments with rockets. Space travel no longer seemed just a dream.

could travel in airless space, above the earth's atmosphere. It would not be easy, for the distances were immense. Earth's nearest neighbour, the moon, is about 230,000 miles away. The sun is about 93 million miles away. As for the stars, they are so far away that their distance is measured not in miles, but in light years–the number of miles light travels in a year. Light travels 186,000 miles a second, or more than 6 thousand million miles a year. And the nearest star, Alpha Centauri, is more than four light years away. A rocket moving at 25,000 miles an hour would not reach Alpha Centauri for 120,000 years.

Reaching the stars was too much to hope for. But the right kind of rocket, with the right kind of fuel, might reach the moon.

During the 1940's, experiments with rockets were made at the German Research Institute at Pennemunde. These experiments led to the development of the V-2, which the Germans used in World War II. The Americans sent a captured V-2 up 114 miles, and did even better with rockets of their own. The Viking reached an altitude of 135 miles. In 1949 a two-stage rocket, a combination of a V-2 and an American made Wac-Corporal, was sent to a height of 240 miles–an unbelievable distance for those days.

As the experiments went on, rockets went higher and higher. The Jupiter-C reached 625 miles in 1956, and the following year the Farside went 2,700 miles. New types of materials, new types of fuel were tested. In Russia, too, scientists were busy testing rockets. Like the Americans, they were planning to launch satellites–small artificial moons that would revolve around the earth.

Men were ready for the adventure of space.

Terrestrial Space

Exosphere

Farside

Jupiter-C

Ionosphere

V-2 Plus Wac-Corporal

Viking

V-2

Stratosphere

Paths taken around the earth by the first eight satellites:
1. Sputnik I launched Oct. 4, 1957; fell Jan. 4, 1958 **2.** Sputnik II launched
Nov. 3, 1957; fell April 14, 1958 **3.** Explorer I launched Jan. 31, 1958
4. Vanguard launched March 17, 1958; probable life, about 200 years
5. Explorer III launched March 26, 1958; fell June 27, 1958 **6.** Sputnik III
launched May 15, 1958 **7.** Explorer IV launched July 26, 1958; fell
Oct. 22, 1959 **8.** Atlas launched Dec. 18, 1958; fell Jan. 21, 1959

THE AGE OF SPACE BEGINS

Thousands of Americans leaned a little closer to their radios, listening to the voice of the announcer.

'Listen now,' he was saying, 'for the sound which forever more separates the old from the new'.

A moment later, there was the sound itself–a thin, high *beep . . . beep . . . beep*. For only a few days earlier, on October 4, 1957, Russian scientists had launched the first man-made earth satellite from a carrier rocket. Like a tiny moon, it was circling the world, sending signals from its radio transmitter: *beep . . . beep . . . beep . . . beep*. Men had taken their first leap into space, and the Space Age had begun.

The satellite was called 'Sputnik', a Russian word meaning 'fellow-traveller'. It was a hollow globe made of aluminium and other metals. It measured 22.835 inches in diameter and weighed 184.3 lb. To keep the

temperature inside the globe at the right point, it was filled with circulating nitrogen gas. Besides the radio, the satellite carried instruments to register information on the outside temperature and other space conditions by changes in the radio signals.

Radio receiving stations throughout the world picked up the sputnik's *beep . . . beep . . . beep*, tracing the satellite's path around the earth. Sky-watchers with telescopes or binoculars peered at the heavens, hour after hour. At dawn or dusk they finally caught sight of the sputnik. Reflecting the light of the sun, it shone out against the darkness like a pale star. It was about 560 miles above the earth, travelling at a speed of 18,000 miles an hour and circling the globe once every 96.2 minutes. And travelling with the sputnik were parts of the third-stage rocket and the protective cone.

For three weeks the sputnik sent out its message from space, until the battery of the radio went dead. Silently it continued its flight, coming closer and closer to earth. At last, during the first week of 1958, it fell into the earth's atmosphere. As it rushed through the air, friction made it glow with heat. Turning fiery red, then white, it broke into pieces and was quickly burned to dust. By this time the sputnik had travelled more than 37,000,000 miles and had made about 1,400 trips around the earth. And by this time, too, another sputnik was whirling through space—carrying a passenger.

The second sputnik was launched on November 3, 1957. Unlike the first, it was shaped like a cone, and was itself the third stage of a three-stage rocket. It weighed 1,120 lb., and in its nose was a little dog named Laika. Chemicals furnished her with oxygen to breathe, and she was fed by automatic equipment. As Laika rode through space, information about her breathing, heartbeat, and blood pressure was sent to earth by radio. On November 10 the signals stopped, and a few days later scientists were sure the little dog was dead.

But Sputnik 2 went on circling the earth, and on January 31, 1958, it was joined by a companion— Explorer I, the first American satellite. Up from Cape Canaveral in Florida, with a great roar and a burst of flame, rose a U.S. Army Jupiter-C rocket. The fourth stage of the rocket and the satellite went into orbit as one bullet-shaped unit. The Explorer was small; it was 80 inches long, 6 inches in diameter, and weighed 30.8 lb. But its tiny instruments immediately began gathering information on space. Instead of the *beep . . . beep . . . beep* of the sputniks, it spoke in a sort of musical hum, telling the world about cosmic rays and meteorite particles, and other phenomena of space.

Sputnik II carried a passenger – Laika, a dog. She is shown here in her compartment, which was placed inside the satellite.

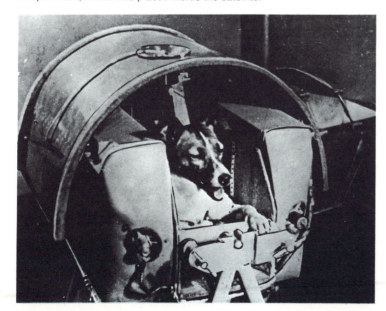

Sputnik I, first of the man-made satellites.

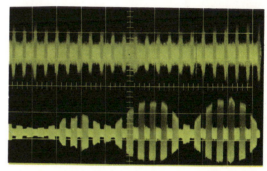

The sounds of Sputnik I (below) and Sputnik II (at top) shown on an oscilloscope, a device that changes sound waves to patterns of light which are recorded on a screen.

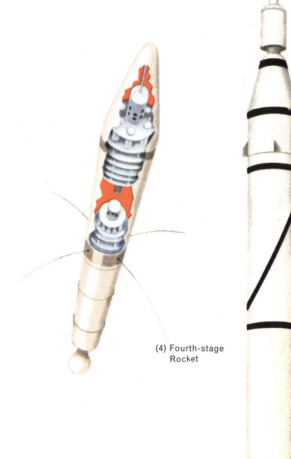

(1) Antenna

(2) Instruments

(3) Nose cone

(4) Fourth-stage Rocket

Explorer I, America's first satellite, and the four-stage Jupiter C rocket that launched it into orbit.

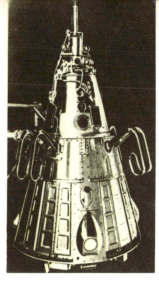

Explorer 4 leaves its launching pad. This was specially designed to investigate the mysterious Van Allen radiation belts surrounding the earth, first detected by America's Explorer I satellite.

Sputnik III, sixth satellite to go into orbit.

SATELLITES IN SPACE

First there was Sputnik I, then Sputnik 2, then Explorer I. And on March 17, 1958, the second American satellite began its journey. It was named Vanguard, after the U.S. Navy's three-stage rocket that sent it on its way. Vanguard was an aluminium globe measuring 6.4 inches in diameter and weighing 3.25 lb. The smallest of the first four satellites, it went farthest – 2,466 miles from earth at the apogee, or highest point, of its orbit. It will have a long life, too. Scientists estimated that it could remain in space for about 200 years.

Since these early days hundreds and hundreds of satellites have been launched. Big, heavy, satellites; small, light, satellites; long, thin, satellites; short, squat, satellites and satellites that change their shape while in orbit.

The satellites have carried an amazing range of instruments and measuring devices. These instruments have measured the temperature of space, the pressure of space, the radiation in space, the radiation from the sun and the magnetic field surrounding the earth. They have measured X-rays and the cosmic rays coming from outer space.

Some satellites have carried cameras to photograph the clouds covering the earth. These are the weather satellites and are among the most useful satellites of all. Although the first crude 'pictures' of the earth's clouds were sent back by America's Vanguard 2 satellite launched in February 1959, the first really successful weather satellite was Tiros I, launched in April, 1960.

While out of range of the ground station, the satellite recorded up to 32 photographs on storage tape for later transmission to the ground. This permitted pictures to be taken on the other side of the world and then transmitted to stations in the United States.

Although Tiros I was only an experimental device, by the time its batteries faded after 78 days, over 22,000 photographs had been transmitted. These pictures revolutionised our knowledge of the earth's cloud cover. The cloud systems are more highly organised than was thought and some formations extend for thousands of miles.

Weather satellites are now permanently in orbit. The picture-taking systems have been simplified and can now be received by relatively cheap equipment that can be installed almost anywhere. Meteorologists study the pictures received and use the information to improve their daily weather forecasts. Day in, day out, silent and invisible, the weather satellites circle the earth above our heads fulfilling their important task.

Also silent and invisible are the communications satellites. These now play so common a part in everyday long distance communications that we take them for granted. But before 1958 there were no communications satellites.

The first one was Score-Atlas, which broadcast a Christmas message from President Eisenhower in 1958. Most famous of the early communications satellites, however, was Telstar, which was used for a series of exciting test television programmes between America and Europe, across the Atlantic in July 1962.

Telstar had one big drawback. Because television and radio signals travel in straight lines, it could only be used when it was in view simultaneously of the transmitting and receiving stations in the U.S. and Europe. When it was 'below the horizon' it could not be used.

The higher the orbit, the longer a satellite remains visible and the Russians place their Molniya communications satellites in highly elongated orbits that take their high points—the apogee—thousands of miles above the earth. In this way, the satellites can be used to transmit messages and radio and television programmes for many hours during each orbit.

Scientists, however, have long known that if a satellite were placed into orbit 22,300 miles above the surface, its orbital speed would be such that it would take exactly one day to make each orbit. It would thus keep pace with the rotation of the earth and would appear to remain motionless in the sky above the same spot on a map. This is the orbit used by most of the United States' communications satellites.

The first commercial communications satellite, that is, the first one intended for everyday business telephone calls, newspaper reports, and television programmes, was launched in April, 1965. Known as Early Bird, this could handle 240 telephone conversations at once and represented an extremely important step in the progress of satellites in space.

One of the smallest satellites ever launched, Vanguard I, functioned for several years, obtaining power from its solar cells.

Picture of the weather over Britain received from the American ESSA-2 meteorological satellite. Such pictures can be received almost anywhere on earth, using relatively cheap and simple equipment.

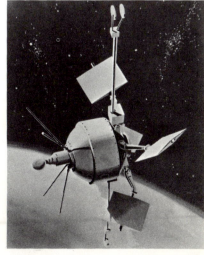

Ariel, Britain's first satellite. It was launched by an American rocket.

First man to travel through space was Yuri Gagarin, who went into orbit in Vostok I on April 12, 1961. The picture on the left shows the ball-like spaceship attached to the rocket stage which gave it the final kick into space.

MAN IN SPACE

Having learnt how to put satellites into orbit, and found out from experiments with animals that creatures could live in space, it was only a matter of time before man himself went into space.

Nevertheless the moment when it came was exciting and historic. Launched in the spacecraft Vostok 1 on 12 April, 1961, the Russian cosmonaut Yuri Gagarin reported 'I saw for the first time the earth's spherical

John Glenn photographed during his flight in space in the Mercury Spacecraft Friendship 7.

shape. You can see its curvature when looking to the horizon. You can see the impressive transition from the bright surface of the earth to the completely black sky in which you can see the stars. The range of transition is a thin one, like a film or narrow belt girdling the globe. It is a soft light-blue colour and the entire transition from blue to black is smooth and beautiful.'

This occasion was undoubtedly one of the great moments in the history of mankind. A centuries old dream became reality. For the first time man had gone into space.

Gagarin spent 90 minutes in orbit. The first man to spend a whole day in space was Herman Titov, another cosmonaut, as the Russians call their astronauts.

The first American astronaut was John Glenn, who made three orbits round the earth in the Mercury spacecraft, Friendship 7, in February, 1962. The first woman to go into space was Valentina Tereschkova. While in orbit in the spaceship Vostok 6, she passed close to her fellow cosmonaut Bykovsky, who had been launched into space in Vostok 5 two days previously.

In March 1965 one of the most exciting moments in the exploration of space took place. While in orbit in the spaceship Voshkod 2, cosmonaut Leonov opened the hatch, and stepped outside into the empty loneliness of space itself. Tethered to the spaceship by a sixteen-foot long lifeline, he whirled through the vacuum at 18,000 m.p.h. For ten minutes Leonov gazed down at the earth and then climbed back inside the Voshkod to join his commander. In addition to being a brave act, Leonov's feat was important as it showed that man could leave the safety of a spaceship. This will be necessary in the future, when large space stations are assembled in orbit.

Within a few weeks of Leonov's exploit, the American astronaut, Edward White, also 'walked' in space. While outside the Gemini spaceship, White practised moving about with the aid of a jet gun, which squirted tiny spurts of gas when the trigger was squeezed.

The two-man Gemini spacecraft were used for long duration flights of four, eight and fourteen days, confirming that man could stay in space at least long enough to travel to the moon and back. The Gemini spacecraft were also used for an important series of rendezvous and docking experiments, experience of which was needed to help further America's plan to land two men on the moon.

Edward White 'walking' in space. While outside his Gemini spacecraft, White used a jet-gun to help him move about.

Rendezvous in orbit. This photograph of Gemini 7 was taken through a window on Gemini 6 while orbiting 160 miles above the earth on December 15, 1965. Gemini 7 was crewed by astronauts Frank Borman and James Lovell, who later became the first men to go round the moon, together with William Anders.

Spectacular picture of the crater Langrenus taken from the Apollo 8 spacecraft while in orbit around the moon on December 24th, 1968. Langrenus has a central peak and conspicuous terraces on the inner crater.

Lunar Orbiter spacecraft.

REACHING FOR THE MOON

After men had launched satellites they began to think seriously of visiting their nearest neighbour in space—the moon. No longer was it quite the fantastic dream it had been previously. Newspapers and magazines carried stories and pictures explaining what the trip would be like, sometimes indicating that it would be no more difficult than flying across the Atlantic.

Scientists knew better. They needed more facts before the Columbus of space could set out on the first historic voyage. And they would get the facts by sending up unmanned rockets.

The first attempt to reach the moon was made on

Replicas of the emblems of the U.S.S.R. carried to the moon by Luna 2.

October 11, 1958, when the U.S. Air Force launched Pioneer 1. But the rocket misfired and only reached an altitude of 71,000 miles before falling back into the atmosphere and burning up. Pioneer 3 also fell back into the atmosphere.

Near success came when Russia launched Luna 1 a few weeks later. This passed within 4,700 miles of the moon and went on to become the first artificial planet in orbit round the sun. Luna 2, launched on September 12, 1959, hit the moon two days later. An astounding feat of rocket marksmanship, this was the first time a man-made object had reached another body in space.

Luna 3, launched in October 1959, went behind the moon and televised the first ever pictures of the rear face which is always turned away from the earth.

For the next five years scientists tried unsuccessfully to obtain further information on the moon, America with a series of Ranger spacecraft, and Russia with another five Luna craft.

Success came to America with Ranger 7. Before this craft crashed into the moon, it sent back 4,316 pictures of the surface, including the first ever close-ups of the surface. The pictures showed much more detail than had previously been obtainable through earth telescopes. Later Rangers sent back further pictures of other areas of equal interest and value.

Luna 9 spacecraft.

Historic close-up picture of the surface of the moon, taken by Luna 9. This showed the surface to have a pumicestone-like appearance and to be almost dust free.

To obtain further information on the nature of the lunar soil, Surveyor 3 carried a scoop which could be extended five feet to dig narrow trenches up to 18 inches deep.

One of the major unknowns of the moon at this time concerned the nature of the surface. One popular theory suggested that it was covered with a deep layer of dust, into which spaceships and astronauts would sink without trace. This unhappy thought was disproved by Russia's Luna 9 spacecraft. On February 3, 1966, this landed gently on the surface and sent back the first real close-up pictures of the surface. These showed that it was virtually dust free and had a pumice-stone-like appearance.

The findings of Luna 9 were confirmed by other Luna spacecraft, and by America's series of Surveyors. Luna 13, which landed in December 1966, carried special equipment to determine the firmness and density of the surface. One of the instruments, mounted at the end of a long arm, forced a test rod into the ground to determine its firmness.

While Lunas and Surveyors were obtaining facts about the surface, America's series of Lunar Orbiter spacecraft were engaged in photographing almost the entire surface of the moon, to help find a suitable area where safe landings by astronauts could be attempted. Fitted with special cameras these spacecraft took the best photographs of the surface of the moon obtained up to that time. These enabled a map of the moon to be prepared which in some ways is more accurate than the maps we have of the earth itself!

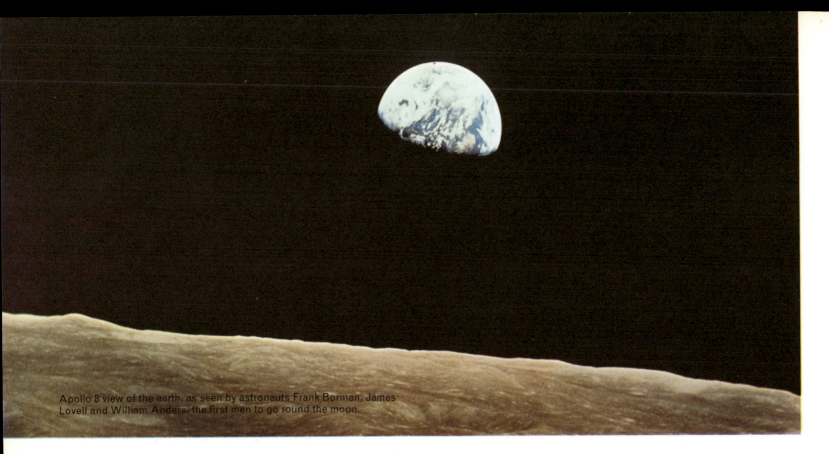

Apollo 8 view of the earth, as seen by astronauts Frank Borman, James Lovell and William Anders, the first men to go round the moon.

MAN ON THE MOON

'I believe that this nation should commit itself to achieving the goal, before this decade is out, of landing a man on the moon and returning him safely to the earth', declared John F. Kennedy, then President of the United States, in May, 1961.

Everybody knew that it would be a tremendous task, requiring the highest skills of almost all branches of technology, ranging from metallurgy to engineering, from electronics to chemistry. It would also require supreme courage from the astronauts who would take part in this the greatest of all man's adventures. President Kennedy appreciated this and at the beginning commented that of all the space projects of this period 'none will be so difficult or expensive to accomplish'. His assessment was correct.

Recovery of Apollo 8 after its historic journey round the moon.

But, eight years later, the moon spaceship was ready. Named Apollo, it had been thoroughly tested over and over again. First of all a number of unmanned craft were tested in space. They worked perfectly.

Then Apollo 7 was sent into orbit round the earth carrying three astronauts. It stayed up a week – the time it would take to get to the moon and back – and then landed safely.

Apollo 8, launched just before Christmas 1968, went out to and circled the moon ten times without landing, and then returned to earth safely. This was the first time in history that men had been so close to the moon and they saw details never before seen. They saw the back of the moon, which always faces away from the earth. While the craft circled the moon at a height of 70 miles, pictures of the surface were televised to earth so that viewers could join in the excitement.

Apollo 9 was sent into orbit to test the Lunar Module, the portion of the spacecraft that would actually land on the moon. Apollo 10 was a full dress rehearsal for the actual landing, with the crew examining the landing site and testing the spacecraft as they orbited the moon.

Then, in July 1969, Apollo 11 took off, perched on top of its mighty Saturn launching rocket, with a noise that could be heard twenty-five miles away. The Apollo spacecraft was first put into a parking orbit round the earth, so that its systems could be thoroughly checked. All was well, and so the motor was fired to start the astronauts, Neil Armstrong, Michael Collins and Edwin Aldrin on the quarter-million mile journey to the moon. On the way the spaceship detached itself from the top of the third stage of the Saturn launching rocket, turned round and then extracted the Lunar Module, which for the take-off had nestled inside the rocket.

Reaching the moon, Apollo went into orbit round it. Once again all the systems and equipment were carefully checked. Then Armstrong and Aldrin left the main cabin and crawled into the spider-like Eagle. After checking its systems, it was detached from the mother-craft and started on the descent to the surface. Lower and lower it descended, slowed by its powerful rocket motor. Then, amid a flurry of smoke and dust, it settled gently on the surface.

After landing, the astronauts carefully checked their craft to ensure that no damage had been caused by the landing. Then, after a meal and a rest, at four minutes to four on the morning of July 21, 1969, Neil Armstrong opened a small hatch in the side of the Eagle and climbed down a ladder attached to one of the landing legs. Man was on the moon.

Saturn V rocket used to launch Apollo.

The Apollo II Lunar Module on the moon's surface, soon after its historic landing in July 1969. Passengers were astronauts Armstrong and Aldrin.

INDEX

Credits

Position Key: L left, R right, T top, B bottom

Photographs: Bendix Aviation Corp., 75 far L, T L; Boeing Airplane Company, endpapers, 65 B, 74 B; British Information Services, 25 B R; Brown Brothers, 12 L, 28 B L, 33 T L, 34 B L, 40 T, 42, 44, 48 TL, BL, BR; Culver Service, 17, 36, 47, 48 TR, 49; Fairchild Aerial Surveys, 53 L; FPG, 55; Gelman Collection, 80 B L, R; Imperial War Museum, 34 T R, 37 B R; Institute of Aeronautical Sciences, 12 R, 28 T, 33 B L, R, 40 B, 77; Kollsman Instrument Corp., 75 B L, R column; Library of Congress, 34 T L; Museum of Modern Art, 80 T R, 81; NACA, 66; NASA, 86 B L, 87, 88, 90, 91; Smithsonian Institution, 30, 46; Sovfoto, 83 B L, 84; UPI, 13, 34 T L, 41, 53 R; Wide World, 83 R; Ziff-Davis Pub. Co., 80 B L.

Art Sources: p. 19 (Lilienthal glider), Culver Service; p. 43 (mid-air refuelling), Historical Collection, Union Title Insurance Company, San Diego, California; p. 48 (Lt. Doolittle's aeroplane), Wide World; p. 76 (Fort McHenry), Stokes Collection, N.Y. Public Library.

Our special thanks to Miss Elizabeth Brown of the Institute of Aeronautical Sciences, Mr Douglas Rolfe, Hawker Siddeley and the Information Services of the U.S. Air Force, Army and Navy for their kind co-operation and generous help.